FROM THE LIBRARY OF

Gladys far left, Margaret far right, their father top centre at Mary Alice Duley's marriage to Edward Jefferies in 1911 in England. The bride is the Aunt Alice of the Somerset letters.

Margaret Duley:
Newfoundland Novelist
A Biographical and Critical Study

by
Alison Feder

Harry Cuff Publications Limited
St. John's, Newfoundland, Canada
1983

Appreciation is expressed to the *Canada Council* and the *Newfoundland &* *Labrador Arts Council* for publication assistance.

Printed in Canada by
CREATIVE PRINTERS & PUBLISHERS LTD.
803 Water Street, St. John's, Newfoundland

ISBN 0-919095-41-0

For
David and Herb

Alison Feder, a Newfoundlander, is Professor of English at Memorial University, St. John's. Her special areas of teaching and research are Victorian Literature and modern Anglo-Irish literature. She has co-edited, with Bernice Schrank, the book **Literature and Folk Culture: Ireland and Newfoundland**. *Author of various critical articles and reviews she has now turned to biography and to deepening her study of Newfoundland writers.*

CONTENTS

I shall blossom like a dark pansy, and be delighted
there among the dark sun-rays of death.
I can feel myself unfolding in the dark sunshine of death
to something flowery and fulfilled, and with a strange sweet perfume.

D. H. Lawrence, "Gladness of Death."

Preface

The purpose of this study is to provide a life of the Newfoundland novelist, Margaret Duley (1894-1968), together with an analysis of her work, and to describe the social milieu that was both her home and her inspiration.

The documentary sources from which the biography has been constructed are described in the first section of the bibliography. There are gaps in the evidence. It is possible, nevertheless, through the co-operation of many people, to produce a portrait with some light and shade. My greatest debt is to members of the author's family: Florence, Mrs. Cyril Duley, sister-in-law; Margot, Mrs. Lance Morrow, niece; Gladys, Mrs. Jefferson Courtney, sister; Margaret, Mrs. George Crowell, niece; Marshall Courtney, nephew, and his wife Delia; Freda, Gwen, and Nora Jefferies, first cousins.

I wish to thank especially Memorial University of Newfoundland for giving me sabbatical leave to work on the book; Dr. D. G. Pitt, Head of the English department, for particular co-operation; G. M. Story for continual encouragement and for reading the manuscript; Paulette Evans for patience and care in typing various drafts; Cathy Murphy for additional typing; and Betty Miller for the final typescript.

In the text that follows I have not changed Margaret Duley's punctuation or spelling except in her last letters where it is obvious that her palsied fingers continually strike the wrong typewriter keys. Also, since she often seems to quote from memory, I have not generally corrected errors in her biblical and literary allusions.

Alison Feder
Memorial University of Newfoundland
May, 1983

CHAPTER ONE

Margaret's Parents

Margaret Duley was influenced in important ways by the diverging personalities of her mother and father. Her dominating mother almost certainly diminished the self-confidence of her daughter and aided to some extent the inertia that cut short her career as a novelist. At the same time, her gentle father was unable to teach her the toughness that she would need to withstand the vagaries of the publishing world when she began to write. As a result, her sensitivity to criticism and her well-masked shyness were to a considerable degree learned from her parents.

There were five children in the Duley family: Cyril Chancey, born 24 May 1890; Nelson Montgomery, born 31 October 1892; Gladys Mildred, born 28 March 1893; Margaret Iris, born 27 September 1894; and Lionel Thomas, born 3 December 1897.

Their mother, Tryphena Chancey Soper, the fifth child of John Soper and Julia Wilkinson, was born on Christmas Day 1866 at Carbonear, Conception Bay, Newfoundland. Tryphena's father was entered in the parish register of births as a planter and later as a fisherman. Whether he suffered a fall in fortunes is difficult to say, especially since the nice distinctions of the words planter, fisherman, planter-fisherman and planterman are too complex to explore in this study because they range from the fisherman with the smallest catch to the owner of a vessel who went fishing with his crew and shared the profits with them, and extend even to the varieties of merchants who owned several vessels and sent them as far as Labrador. In addition, there is nothing to indicate that John Soper practised his profession on a large scale. He is certainly not a legend in Carbonear, and although Tryphena never denied her forebears, she is not known to have taken any special pride in them. In fact, she took pains to prevent a class-conscious St. John's from thinking of her as only a fisherman's daughter. Mr. Soper, who drowned on 13 January 1879 at the age of fifty-six and left his widow with seven children, remains a shadowy figure — for no amount of probing has enabled me to bring him to life.

It has also been impossible to discover much about Julia Soper, Margaret

Duley's maternal grandmother, apart from the fact that she lived a long life and was reputed to possess the psychic power known as "second sense." Her headstone in the small Methodist graveyard on the South Side of Carbonear is inscribed "In loving memory of Julia Soper, who died 4 September 1916 aged 90."

Julia Soper's sister, Margaret Parnel Wilkinson, had married Lionel Thomas Chancey in St. John's in December 1853, and years later she and her husband, still childless, adopted Tryphena Soper, and brought her to St. John's, where she lived with them until her marriage to Thomas Duley in 1899. Brought up with her was another niece, Laura Christian, who became another adopted daughter, and later married John Currie, the owner of the St. John's newspaper, the *Daily News*. She was the Auntie Loll referred to affectionately in Margaret Duley's letters.

Why or when Julia Soper relinquished one of her girls to her sister remains unknown. It might have been before her husband's death; more likely it was afterwards, when the strain of a large family and widowhood were great. At any rate, there was nothing singular in allowing a younger child to go to a loving relative in the city, where the social and educational advantages would be greater. Situated less than a hundred miles from St. John's, Carbonear was easily accessible from the city; and, in fact, there is evidence that Tryphena Soper brought her children to the attractive sea-port town for their summer holidays. "Townies" though they were, they learned a lot about outport life and the fishing industry.[1] Some of the older members of the community remember that Tryphena went frequently to see her sister Mary Ann, who married Segar Pike of Carbonear; but they do not mention her mother. Whether Julia Soper lived with Mary Ann or in a house of her own is conjectural. In fact, her life is so invisible one wonders if there is a mystery somewhere. Was she mentally unbalanced? Was she in an institution? Was she the grandmother who, Margaret Duley said, was the model for Mrs. Slater in *Highway to Valour*? Or was this grandmother Julia Sopher's sister, the Margaret Chancey who adopted Tryphena? Perhaps. But why then did the Duley children call her Great Aunt Chancey and not Grandmother? Margaret Chancey would have been an accessible grandmother figure to Margaret Duley, since they lived close by each other, but the character in the novel could certainly be a recollection of Julia Soper. If so, she was a wise, serene, enduring woman whose godliness was more than mere lip-service. There was also, perhaps, something of Julia Soper in *Cold Pastoral* in the character of Josephine Keilly, the outport mother, who not only has the "second sense" but also allows her daughter, Mary Immaculate, to be adopted by a city family and spared the harsh realities of "the Cove." Although the circumstances were changed and the Keilly family was Catholic, the home life with seven children bore some resemblance to the fishing background of the Carbonear Sopers with their seven children.

This Soper-Chancey-Duley connection, which had been established by the union of Lionel Thomas Chancey and Margaret Parnel Wilkinson, was a long and happy one, for they were a generous, loving couple. Although the Chanceys had a house on Freshwater Road, they were probably living at 7 Monkstown Road when Tryphena came to live with them. The large house, with its pretty side verandah, is still occupied and in good condition, although its situation is now marred by traffic islands and parking lots in the area of Rawlins Cross.

The new daughter was brought up in a strong, Congregationist atmosphere. Someone who knew her told me that Mrs. Chancey was "the greatest bigot that ever lived." The charges and counter charges of bigotry must have fallen as thick as hailstones in the days when ecumenism was virtually unknown and a rigid conformity to rules made people feel spiritually safe and free to turn up their noses at religions different from their own. Mr. Chancey was a teetotaller and a devoted member of his church. The household seemes to have been a cultivated one because Lionel Thomas had bookish interests: "He began work as a compositor for the *Morning Courier* and later, in partnership with a Man called Chisholm, had a Book & Stationery business."[2] In addition to being sub-sheriff of St. John's from 1867 to 1899, he seems to have acquired a good deal of property. Judging from the details of his will with its bequests of money and real estate, he was a well-to-do man. References by the Duleys to Great Aunt Chancey's silver, and to various things they had inherited, indicate that their mother was surrounded by the good things of life in a handsomely equipped house.

Tryphena Soper probably attended the Congregational stone chapel on Queen's Road until it was destroyed by the Great Fire of 1892, and afterwards the new wooden one that was built on the same site. Although little is known about her early schooling, it is likely that she went to the St. John's Training School established in 1874 by Emily and Matilda Good for pupil-teachers. This establishment was in the basement of the church for the first year, but it was moved to a large house on Monkstown Road the next. Here in June, 1886, Tryphena received a Government Certificate First Grade, which qualified her to teach at the training school. She seems to have been clever, for she became assistant to the new principal, Miss Cox, who advertised the course of studies and fees in 1886 as follows: "Fees from $1.00 to $2.50 per term with an extra charge of $1.00 for Latin, Greek, Book-keeping or Painting."[3] Tryphena was thus educated as a young lady of the leisure class of her time. In addition, her fine singing voice made her a popular performer at many public concerts.

Although the details of her meeting and courtship with T. J. Duley are unclear, it is probable that they met through their activities in the Congregational Church. Perhaps he heard her sing "Golden Love" in March 1886 at an entertainment in aid of the Organ Fund, a programme which inexplicably allowed the choir to sing "Cruiskeen Lawn," which, translated from the Irish, means "little overflowing jug." There was something incongruous about Miss Soper, the future scourge of bacchanalians and the leading light of the local branch of the Women's Christian Temperance Union, countenancing a glee in

9

which the singers shamelessly invoked the "immortal and divine Great Bacchus" as their adopted father and promised in his honour never to let their glasses run dry. In spite of the dangers of such libation-songs, Tryphena and Tom pursued their interest in music so that he had become choirmaster by 1895. The two were married on 31 July 1889 when she was twenty-two and he was twenty-seven.

Thomas James Duley was born in Birmingham, England, on 29 July 1862 and died on 13 January 1920 at the age of fifty-seven. His parents were Charles Duley of Manchester, England, and Hannah Lawrence of Tipperary, Ireland. Thomas Duley arrived in St. John's in 1883 to work with the jewellery firm of Ohman, Lindstrom and Northfield. When this triumvirate separated, Duley joined Mr. Ohman, but subsequently started his own business on the site of the Pitts Building on Water Street. After the fire of 1892, he moved to a store on the north side of the same street and built up the large and successful firm of T. J. Duley, in which he was assisted by his sons Cyril and Nelson when they were old enough. Not only did T. J. Duley and Company live up to their soubriquet, "The Reliable Jewellers," but their monogrammed boxes and cases, which were lined with white satin, were as distinctive as the Henry Birks "blue boxes" of today.

Thomas Duley appears to have been a quiet man, who was liked by everyone. Uninterested in society or social climbing, he immersed himself in the activities of the Congregational Church. As a prominent Mason, he held several important positions. He was also a longtime member of the Bible Society and in general worked for the moral and civic good of St. John's. His obituary notices indicate that he was a courageous and religious man.[4] His illness was very brief; and Margaret Duley was always glad that he was spared lingering pain. She wrote a kind of epitaph for him years later in 1953 in a letter to Aunt Alice Jefferies, her father's sister: "I know very well that he was an angel of a father."

Glimpses of his personality may be seen in the recollections of the family. His daughter Gladys Duley Courtney recalled vividly an episode that occurred when she and her younger sister were playing after tea in the front yard of the home on Freshwater Road, where their parents first lived after their marriage. Loud, bawdy singing in the road sent the children flying into the house crying, "Da-da, here comes Breezer O'Brien and he's coming fast." When the drunken Breezer reached the house, he took out a long, black-handled knife, leaned over the fence and called out, "Duley, Mr. Duley, I'm coming for you and I'm going to let your blood." In spite of the little girls' terror for his safety, Duley went to the gate to confront Breezer, who, after pouring out a river-flood of threats, finally quietened down, and went off on his long cart, trusting to his horse, who was well used to his master's ways, to lead him home.

Mrs. Courtney thought that this incident might be a source for the aversion to blood-letting that ran through her sister's novels. It could, indeed, be reflected in Mageila Michelet's fainting spells in *Highway to Valour*, when she sees the interlocked antlers of two stags' heads in her grandfather's house, and when she is served a large bullock's heart for dinner, or when she reads about the Crucifixion. In addition, Trevor Morgan's shielding of Mageila from the bloody sights at the whaling station in Labrador may have a similar origin, as may David FitzHenry's hatred of the seal hunt in *Cold Pastoral*. Other explanations for Margaret Duley's aversion to blood may be found in her attitude to war, which had wounded or snatched away those dear to her; as well as in her memory of her brother Nelson hemorrhaging as a victim of both tuberculosis and alcoholism. Years after his death, she told two friends that she actually shovelled blood from the floor of his room. Allowing for exaggeration, her close association with Nelson as he manifested the symptoms of advanced cirrhosis of the liver led to her a life-long fear of bleeding.

After Lionel's birth, the Duleys moved from Freshwater Road to 51 Rennies Mill Road, a more prestigious address, which they named "Lozells" after the house in Birmingham of Thomas' Great Aunt Hare, his mother's sister. While the growing family prompted this move, it was probably hastened by Mrs. Duley, who seems to have been anxious to move up in the social world. Meanwhile, Mrs. Hare had taken a great interest in all ten of her sister's children and had even adopted Alice, who appears as "Auntie Alice" in Margaret Duley's correspondence with her English relatives. It was from Mr. Hare, who was an art dealer in Birmingham, that Mr. Duley learned about good pictures, hung them on his walls, and probably encouraged Margaret's interest in art and her tentative attempts at painting.

Many people in St. John's still remember Thomas Duley as a tall, good-looking, unassuming man who was often seen walking to his store or driving out in his carriage. As unaffected as he was, Duley wished, nevertheless, to see his daughters well settled; for example, he urged Margaret to marry Herbert Brookes, his personal friend, whom he made one of the co-executors of his will. Brookes was a widower who seemed to Duley to be ideally suited to his daughter; for he was English, a Congregationalist, an Associate of the Society of Incorporated Accountants and Auditors of London, England, and of the Institute of Chartered Accountants of Nova Scotia; and, in addition, he held directorships in several well-known firms. But Margaret Duley, who was thirteen years younger than Brookes, was not interested in him romantically, so that she refused his proposal of marriage, in spite of the fact that her mother also pressed her to accept.

According to one acquaintance, Mrs. Duley was "a presence, my dear, a presence." Haughty, matriarchal and puritanical, she was also imaginative, jolly, and kind. She was "Phenie" to those who liked her, and to those who did not she was "Duchess of Dishwater" (pronounced waw-tah). This appellation originated in the skit which the wartime entertainers, "The Dumb-bells," performed at the old Casino Theatre on Henry Street in St. John's some time after the Armistice in 1918. Two friends in the audience nudged one another when a character was named the "Duchess of Dishwater" and one asked the

11

other, "Who does that remind you of?" Thereafter Mrs. Duley was known to many as the duchess; while she herself cultivated the role of *Grande Dame* as much as Mageila's mother does in *Highway to Valour*: "Mama gives orders, Papa makes kind requests." As a novelist, therefore, Margaret Duley seems to recall the essential difference between her parents; for her mother had "high notions," as Newfoundlanders say, and was a bit of a snob. She was a handsome, chesty woman, who went regally to her car, and was driven by a chauffeur called Fowler for much of her married life. The swish of black silk always impressed the Queen's Road congregation when she swept up the aisle with Tom, who rarely had much to say. It must have been clear to Margaret when she was writing *Highway to Valour* that her mother had reared the children to move in select circles.

Meanwhile, Mrs. Duley was indefatigable in church work, just as she often studied the Bible so that she could recite much of it. One story had it that after her death a hundred or more bibles were found in the house. Although this sounds apocryphal, there might well have been a large number because she needed a supply for her bible classes; and perhaps she was a collector of bibles. But in the main, she busied herself with the Ladies' Aid Society and ran teas, bazaars, and dramatic presentations to bring in money for varied Congregational causes like the Organ Fund, the various missions across the island, the Girls' Guild, and the Young Men's Mutual Improvement Society. The Floral Social of February 1913, however, was her great triumph. A contemporary newspaper account paints a vivid picture of the event:

> The Lecture Hall had been tastefully decorated with evergreen and a
> profusion of artificial flowers wonderfully lifelike in colour and form
> . . . a sketch entitled 'Meeting Among the Flowers' was conceived and
> written by Mr. [sic] T. J. Duley . . . Miss Barbara Langmead combined
> dignity and charm as Mother Nature . . . Miss Mildred Thomas as
> Mother Earth. The chrysanthemum of Miss Ethel Barnes was finely
> saucy and the carnation of Miss Belle Russell splendidly arrogant . . .' If
> this sounds all a bit precious let it be noted that it was performed again at
> the Seaman's Institute to an audience of Sealers — this time under the
> more robust title, "Mutiny Among the Flowers."[5]

While rehearsals for such performances were always held at Mrs. Duley's house, Margaret seems to have shown no interest in taking part in them.

On the grimmer side, Mrs. Duley was a ferocious temperance-woman. As the foundress of the Loyal Temperance Legion, she used to march children up and down the basement of the Congregational church as she directed their chants, "Beer saloons must go. Liquor must go." As a woman to be reckoned with, she lived up to her beliefs; and as a consequence she represented the Newfoundland branch of the Women's Temperance Union at a world gathering in Edinburgh in 1900. There is no record of her contribution to this meeting, but her friends were led to believe that she was given a standing ovation in the Scottish capital for her speech.

Margaret Duley apparently never forgot the attitude to alcohol in the Duley home. As late as 1956, she told two friends that after her mother's funeral the family brought up a bottle of red wine from the cellar, where it had lain quietly for years, only to find it had turned to vinegar. It seems that even after her death Mrs. Duley was able to do battle for the temperance cause! This anecdote may be apocryphal, however, for it seems to be contradicted by the recollection of Mary Carew, a long-time maid in the home, that decanters of whiskey were to be seen on the sideboard in the dining room. Perhaps the ban applied only to Mrs. Duley's children. If so, it did not help Nelson, and, as far as I know, the others were not teetotallers. What is noticeable about the story is the fact that Margaret, who was never overnice about describing her own feelings or telling a good yarn, could not resist electrifying her friends with the claim that when the corpse went out the door the bottle came in.

Although Mrs. Duley ran Tom, the marriage seemed to be happy. Tryphena kept a quiet, sombrely decorated, well-regulated house, which was heavy with wine-coloured plush and dark mahogany. There might have been two maids at one time, but in the thirties and forties there was only one full-time girl, with extra help three times a week. The servants worked hard scrubbing floors, polishing silver, carrying Margaret's breakfast tray from a basement kitchen, answering bells, which were everywhere, and hauling buckets of coal up the four-flights of stairs to light fires. With a grate in every room and servants' quarters in the basement, there was much hard work for the servants. The boys, particularly Nelson, were considerate, as they helped the girls with heavy loads, but there was no doubt that, although the servants were treated well enough, they were considered by the family to belong to a lower class. As a result, the servant girls wore blue or green uniforms and white aprons in the morning for housework, and black uniforms, white aprons and caps in the afternoon for opening the door to company, putting the blower to the drawing-room fire, and passing the great silver service. They worked in the house every day of the week, but could go out at night; in addition, they were given Sunday afternoon off, but had to return to serve tea before taking the rest of the night off if nothing further was required of them.

Although Mrs. Duley was in some ways an indulgent mistress, she did not allow at the table idle chit-chat which the maids might overhear. But conversation at the Duley table seems often to have been quite serious; for example, the Reverend Wilfred Butcher, who came to Newfoundland in 1938, and who was often asked to dinner on Sundays, recalled that it was at the Duley house that he first began to realize the serious nature of the international situation. In addition, it was his impression of such occasions that Mrs. Duley "ruled."

Tryphena dabbled in writing and even published a story in booklet form during the First World War. This little book was almost a family affair because T. J. Duley and Company helped pay for it by contributing an advertisement for Waterman's Ideal Fountain Pen, while Margaret wrote the verse epilogue, and perhaps some other parts as well. *A Pair of Grey Socks: Facts and Fancies*, which is "Lovingly dedicated to the Boys of the Newfoundland Regiment", is about two chums, Bob, an Irishman, and Jack, a Newfoundlander, who survive the Gallipoli campaign. Bob falls in love with a photograph of Jack's sister which she has tucked at random into one sock among thousands that are to be shipped to the soldiers overseas. When he is demobilized, Bob goes to Newfoundland, marries his Mary of Sweet Apple Cove; and the two live happily ever after. Apart from the sentimentality and blatant use of coincidence, the story is well written, as it touches the reader with its feeling for terrified boys who are turned into heroes overnight. At the close of the story, Mrs. Duley appends a humorous description of the knitting fever that infected St. John's as she depicts hundreds of women making socks from a new, grey wool which was much softer than the homespun used in the outports for the traditional sock with its white toe, black leg, and white top. These grey socks became "a bond of unity between rich and poor" who had only one thought in mind: to work carefully so that their handiwork would not rub the soldier's feet.

Mrs. Duley was authoritarian to the day of her death on 16 November, 1940. Shortly before this, when the Reverend Mr. Butcher called on her to say good-bye before he left St. John's, she sat up in bed and expressed her anger at his not waiting to conduct her funeral service which she knew to be close at hand.

In her will, Mrs. Duley left her cash, bonds and other investments to Gladys and Margaret, while Cyril and Nelson were bequeathed the business. In addition, Gladys received two sets of china, the hundred-year-old silver service and any silver that might have belonged to great Aunt Chancey. Glady's daughter, Margaret Courtney Crowell, was to be given any jewellery that was of value, while Cyril received the cabinet of silver which "came to me on my silver anniversary" and any furniture that came from Mrs. Chancey. Margaret was also left her mother's linen with the exception of two crocheted table cloths "which are my own work which I wish sent to Gladys," and was to share the house with Gladys Courtney. Any other furniture or household goods were to be divided equally between Cyril and Nelson, or were to be sold as they saw fit. After suggesting that the house be kept intact for at least one year, Mrs. Duley completed her will by offering to her children her "Dear, dear, love and prayers for God's rich blessings upon them."

Although Margaret and Gladys were treated equally in the matter of the house and money, there was a distinct implication in the will that a married daughter was more worthy of gifts than an unmarried one. Even Cyril thought that his younger sister fared rather badly, as he wrote to Gladys: "Quite candidly I don't think Mother was altogether fair to Peg, and here again I must confess surprise that she did not poportion things differently. I know from conversations with her that she had every intention of doing so but we can find no evidence of her having done so."

Although it would be rash to say that there was premeditated partiality on Mrs. Duley's part, especially since nobody knows what discussions she might have had with her children, it was clear that Margaret did not receive many special marks of affection. According to Cyril's letter, however, his mother did give Margaret a valuable coin bracelet some weeks before she died. The disposition of the furniture, silver, and china would help to explain why Margaret had so little when she turned the Rennies Mill Road house into apartments in 1953.

All this suggests that the relationship between Duley and her mother was ambiguous. On the one hand Margaret never forgot her mother's strictness and tactlessness. In addition, she was afraid of her mother when she was young. Consequently, years later, she told a friend that as a tiny child, when her bonnet fell over her eyes while she was sitting on her mother's lap, she was afraid to say she could not see, and sat silently waiting to be reprimanded. It is possible also that she saw the beating Nelson took when his mother allegedly drew blood. Similarly, she vividly remembered her mother sighing, "I have no trouble dressing Gladys but Margaret is so thin and delicate I don't know what to put on her." Such tactless remarks not only illustrate her mother's penchant for the biting phrase but also hint at their negative effects on the author as a child. As late as 1953 Margaret wrote to Aunt Alice describing her birthday celebration and telling her she had gone to see Aunt Lollie who was born on the same date, 27 September, "when, as mother always said, there was a frost that pinched all the lovely autumn flowers." It seems that Margaret felt that her arrival had somehow been responsible for spoiling a good autumn.

On the other hand, however, there was a certain bond between them. Margaret inherited her mother's love of the Bible, as well as her considerable knowledge of wild flowers and of cooking; hence she proudly told Mary Quinn that "Mother" took a night course in something or other with her. Much later Margaret was, according to Cyril, very attentive during Mrs. Duley's last illness, as he wrote to Gladys after the funeral: "Peg has been simply wonderful throughout the whole period, she definitely gave over her whole existence to mother for the past five months and was in constant attendance morning, noon and night. Even the nurses leaned on her and I cannot speak too highly of what she did. The result is that now everything is over, a reaction has set in and she shows signs of the strain she has been through." But Margaret did not devote all of her energies to her mother at this time because she was writing *Highway to Valour* to keep her mind off sickness and death. She was, nevertheless, a dutiful daughter who, according to her close friend Mary Quinn, had "a great respect for parental authority and for her mother's accomplishment." There were probably, however, tensions between a mother who dabbled occasionally in writing and a daughter who was contemplating it as a career. When Margaret later became a successful novelist, her mother may have been a little jealous, for it was noted that she used to shrug off compliments about her daughter's work. It may even be possible that Margaret's reticence about her books sprang from a sense of falling short of her mother's expectations for her. It seems clear, therefore, that Tryphena's influence on the author was important and longlasting.

1. Townies are residents of St. John's as distinct from "baymen" who live in an outport, which is usually a fishing settlement. These regionalisms are generally used good-naturedly; but sometimes they bear social malice.
2. The Dissenting Church of Christ at St. John's, 1775-1975: a history of St. David's Presbyterian Church, St. John's, Newfoundland, n.d., p. 195.
3. Ibid., p. 97.
4. *Evening Telegram* (14 January 1920), p. 4; *Daily News* (14 September 1920), p. 4.
5. *op. cit.*, p. 113.

CHAPTER TWO

Margaret

Margaret Iris Duley, ("Peg") was born in 1894; but little else is known about her early years. Some photographs of the time show her in the midst of her brothers and sisters, who are all dressed in the typical clothing of the late Victorian age. In these pictures the girls are wearing black stockings and black boots with side buttons and seem to be enveloped in yards of material with embroidered frills up to the chin and down to the mid-calf, while the boys look like dwarf grandfathers in breeches, waistcoats, watch chains and formal neckwear. In addition, Lionel, the baby, is dressed like a girl.

Gladys Duley Courtney describes her precocious younger sister at age four as follows:

> I remember when Peg and I were children, we lived next door to a woman named Mrs. B..., wife of a Professor at Bishop Field [sic] College who only half lived in this world — the other half lived in a world of the poets and on a plane of dreams and fancies — but to such a child as Peg — she was like a fairy queen. I was five going on to school age six, so was sent to Miss Tuck's pre-school while Peg spent that year under Mrs. B...'s influence reading poetry and listening to verses from Sheldon, Milton and Whittier, as her three tow-headed boys were called, until she was steeped in unreal, unearthly and lofty phrases from the poets' world. It's no wonder she was unprepared to cope with reality at Miss Tuck's next year.

Margaret was bored at Miss Tuck's school. Apparently on the first day, when Miss Tuck had cut her lunch into small squares, the little girl carefully picked out all the raisins, ate them, rose from her seat, got her hat and coat and walked home. It was not the last time that she was to disconcert her teachers.

Gladys Courtenay also recalls that at the age of four Margaret could recite with gestures and tonal variations the whole of Browning's *The Pied Piper*. According to Gladys' recollections, therefore, the little girl was the star performer at Christmas at the home of Uncle and Aunt Chancey, where she leaned

17

"against Aunt Loll's knee waiting her turn & wriggling impatiently." After she sang out the town council's promise in Browning's poem to pay the piper fifty thousand guilders to rid Hamelin of rats, the whole family of Duleys and Chanceys "could sense an increased tempo of activity while this wisp of a child sitting on the floor facing the fire actually rivalled the leaping flames. But this was only rats and she had so much more of a surprise for them if only they'd listen." She leaped off the floor, went back to Auntie Loll's knee, and gave them the full brunt of the piper's wrath when the mayor refused to pay him the promised amount. She mimed the exodus of the children from Hamelin as they followed the piper to the place where "a wondrous portal opened wide." With dramatic effectiveness, she did not tell of the little lame boy who got left behind, or Browning's moral to Willy at the close. Gladys said that when she came to the line, " 'The door in the mountain-side shut fast,' she always stopped there — nothing could induce any further interest. Now for her reward — a package of sugar-sweet ice cream cookies all for herself & no nonsense about turkey and vegetables as long as she was given an almond cookie."

Gladys' memory is probably faulty in recalling the child's age. Although it was possible that Margaret knew Browning's poem by heart when she was four, it seems more than coincidental that *The Pied Piper of Hamelin* was on the school syllabus for 1907, and that in June of that year, when she was twelve, she answered questions on it in the Preliminary grade examination in English (a public examination of the Council of Higher Education in Newfoundland). Whether Gladys was mistaken or not, the delightful fact is that at sometime as a child her sister gave a precocious recitation of the famous poem.

Margaret was not quite seven when she started reading the Elsie books and began to live in imagination as Elsie Dinsmore's best friend.[1] As a result, Margaret's head was full of her reading; and she often had a book on her lap under her desk at school. All the Duley children went to the old Methodist College on Long's Hill in St. John's. If one fulfilled all the academic requirements, and wrote the examinations for Primary Certificate, Preliminary, Intermediate, and Associate, one could become at the time an Associate of Arts. Margaret appears to have gone only as far as Intermediate, which is approximately equivalent to the Grade Eleven of today. Thus she was not qualified to proceed to the London Matriculation Examination, which was set and graded in London and which gave successful candidates entry to the University of London. Although she won several school prizes — one for a short story about a wedding on horseback — she was not academically ambitious. As a consequence, her formal education ended when she left school in 1910.

Margaret's love of literature and her flair for the dramatic were apparent to her teachers, who, as pleased as they were to have a bright student, seem to have found it difficult to maintain their calm in the face of her wilful, independent approach to poetry. Her sister Gladys, for example, remembered an episode that occurred on a lovely spring day when every child was sent to school in her "figure," (i.e. without a coat; the ultimate social achievement at that time in

Newfoundland seems to have been to be able to go out in one's figure for Easter). Consequently, Gladys reports, "Peg was decked out in a new straw hat, a new blue sailor suit and new boots." Perhaps this kind of sartorial vanity induced intellectual vanity in Margaret; at any rate, her impertinence once caused her considerable difficulty in Miss Dodd's class on Sir Walter Scott. Miss Dodd was a stately six-footer, who was reputed to be the daughter of an earl, a noble connection which did not make the slightest impression on the schoolgirl. When the two argued about the pronunciation of Bothwell Hall in *The Lady of the Lake*, Margaret stood her ground by insisting that her view was correct, so that finally the sorely-tried teacher lost her temper and cried, "Such impertinence, Miss, I have never heard. I am not used to it, and will not have it. Little tragedy Queen! Go home. I will see your father." With that, Margaret marched to the cloakroom, pulled on her new hat, climbed the stairs to the school's higher-level door, which was out of bounds to pupils, and defiantly marched home. She cooled her wrath on the way with five cents worth of licorice from Mrs. Summer's candy shop.

The "little tragedy queen" practised her histrionic arts elsewhere as well, for she loved to act out roles from books. Among the books in the Duley household was *Queechy*, a novel by the American author, Elizabeth Wetherell (Susan Warner), who was popular at that time, when many readers liked their piety and sentimentality well blended.[2] *Queechy* describes the moral development of a girl of thirteen who overflows with sensibility and uplifting aphorisms so that its many characters and passionless love story made it very suitable for the make-believe games of the Duley girls.

It may be useful, therefore, to recall briefly the plot and characters of this novel. The heroine is Fleda Ringgam, an orphan, who lives on a farm called Queechy, a name probably suggested by the historic old house and land at Canaan, New York state, where the Warner children spent their summers. A sprite, who loves animals, flowers, and the woods, Fleda is (to paraphrase her creator) the pure gold that does not tarnish, the true coin, the living plant ever blossoming; she is not the cut, arranged flower. When she loses her grandfather, she wilts like a pale anemone, visits her relatives in Paris, grows up with them, and when they return to America and lose their money, devotes herself to their welfare.

The theme of the book is the notion that the little farm girl has inbred qualities which set her far above those who have been brought up with the advantages of a class conscious society. Fleda's beauty is of the kind usually associated with high breeding and stately homes. She transcends her surroundings so completely that she unwittingly becomes a threat to those mothers who seek husbands for their socially prominent daughters. Her reward is marriage to a handsome carpet-knight who returns to his bible-reading at Queechy's request and is reformed. Although the book is for the most part a moral tract, there are in it some wonderful glimpses of the countryside as well as of London, Paris, and New York, and enough interesting characters to help minimize its sermonizing time.

The book contains, therefore, enough similarities to Duley's second novel, *Cold Pastoral*, to indicate a seminal influence on it. As a result, Queechy and Mary Immaculate have much in common. They are elfin creatures who are both in love with animals and the outdoors; both rise in the world from humble beginnings because of their refined personalities. Queechy wears herself out helping Aunt Lucy; Mary Immaculate devotes herself to Mater. The death of Queechy's cousin Hugh is lingeringly lachrymose; Tim Vincent's death is very similar as Mary Immaculate talks him into the next world. The gossamer texture of Mageila Michelet in *Highway to Valour* also owes something to the faultless and fastidious Queechy. It is to this book too that we can perhaps trace Duley's predilection for fragile heroines, fainting fits, accidents, hospitals, death-bed scenes and other tearful features that pervade her work, in spite of its crackling dialogue and satiric humour. It is clear that she never shed completely the mawkishness of Victorian fiction.

Little else is known of Margaret Duley as a schoolgirl. She made her first trip to England in 1911, when Mr. Duley took her and Gladys to the wedding of his sister, Alice May, to Edward Jefferies in Cheltenham, Gloucestershire, on 5 August. In England again in 1913 to 1914, Margaret went from London to Bristol with her father to visit the Jefferies and to see their babies Gwen and Freda, whom she was not to meet again until 1953. It was during this period that she was enrolled at the London Academy of Music and Dramatic Art, where she took elocution lessons from the well-known Shakespearian reciter, Charles Fry (1846-1928). Fry had built a reputation as a reciter in musical works such as Mendelssohn's *Athalie* and *Antigone and Oedipus*; and, as a result, some established composers wrote special scores for his Shakespearian performances, which eventually developed into costume productions with a complete company. In addition, many of his pupils distinguished themselves on the stage. Apart from Gladys Courtney's note that "Peg chose her own school in England" and "was a student at London Conservatory taking Elocution, Art & Drama," there is little record of this visit to England. Because the London Academy of Music and Dramatic Art was bombed during the Second World War and their records destroyed, I was unable to verify dates, or to find out anything about their programme of studies when Margaret was there. One relative said that her father believed that war was inevitable and so insisted that she come home in 1913; on the contrary, Gladys said she came home in 1917. Perhaps Margaret was involved in the war effort in England in some way. But in any event both sisters seem to have been forgetful concerning dates so that Gladys' memory might well have betrayed her in this instance.

What Margaret intended to do with the education in drama that she received in England is not clear. She never indicated that she wanted to be an actress and did not take part in any of the Congregationalist entertainments her mother arranged, nor in any of the amateur productions at the Casino on Henry Street in St. John's. She apparently did not intend to teach; for that would be like a girl of her class becoming a governess or a sempstress. It is likely that she desired to study away from home in order to keep up with Gladys, who, the records show, attended Lowther College, in Lancashire, (now in Rhyl, North Wales). The head of the College in a letter to me dated October 1978 could supply only the fact that Gladys Mildred Duley's name was included in the school magazine on the leaving list for July 1911. Although the details are scanty, it is clear that the Duleys followed the prestigious ritual of the upper-class Newfoundland families of the time by sending their two daughters to finishing school in England. By such means one could sometimes gain access to the aristocratic circles in St. John's; and Margaret's choice of a school in England had a refreshing sense of the unorthodox about it which at the same time did not bar her from high society at home.

While Margaret's two English sojourns of 1911 and 1913 probably made her more cosmopolitan, they did not prepare her for a career of any sort. For they did not seem to have had any practical results other than giving her the opportunity to recite pieces like Alfred Noyes's "The Highwayman" and to use her controversial English accent, and to appear from time to time "on the stage." Some people recalled "her beautiful voice" articulating the verse as she recited poetry and used a fan for graceful emphasis. "On the stage" meant taking part in what Newfoundlanders called an evening concert and which included songs, recitations, dances, violin and piano solos, and often *tableaux* in which famous personages such as the Princes in the Tower or Peter Pan were represented in handsome costumes. Performers wore evening gowns or tuxedos while singers and elocutionists often hid a tiny notebook in their loosely clasped hands lest they forget their words. "The Road to Mandalay," "The Holy City," "Because," "Phil the Fluter's Ball" and "Dark Rosaleen" were very popular songs of the time. Margaret's restricting herself to the local stage suggests that she either gave up the idea of becoming a serious actress, or was forbidden by her parents to enter the wicked world of the theatre. Elocution lessons in England were, it seems, suitable for young ladies; whereas a career as an actress was not.

While in England, as noted, Margaret acquired a distinct English accent which she never gave up. One informant said drily that when Margaret came home she was so grand "she didn't even know the cat" and "couldn't even remember the currency; she was all pounds, shillings, and pence." Although some felt that her English enunciation was not extreme, the general opinion was that it was a very carefully produced sound which became second nature to her. Such verbal window-dressing earned her a good deal of derision because Newfoundlanders, who were willing to accept rounded vowels from Englishmen, were merciless in their condemnation of the adoption of a distinctly foreign accent by one of their own.

The years 1914 to 1918 were painful for the Duleys. Cyril was badly wounded in the war and Lionel, the youngest of the family, was killed at Kieberg Ridge in 1918. Nelson too suffered his own special kind of wound. He had been declared unfit for service because he had tuberculosis; but he would never offer explanations, so that he was consequently called a coward and sent white feathers. All this had a terrible effect on him as he watched a whole generation of Newfoundlanders being wiped out at Beaumont Hamel, Vimy Ridge, Passchendaele, and on the shores of Gallipoli. Nor was Margaret left untouched. The only happy occurrence of the war years seems to have been Gladys's marriage in 1916 to "her southern gentleman," Jefferson Courtney, who took her to live in Virginia and later North Carolina.

It seems to have been generally accepted that Jack Clift was the love of Margaret Duley's life, although there is no evidence that they were to be married. The son of the lawyer and politician, the Hon. J. Augustus Clift, Jack left St. John's with the First Five Hundred of the Royal Newfoundland Regiment. In 1915 he became a lieutenant in the Scottish regiment, the Queen's Own Highlanders, but in 1916 he was transferred back to the Newfoundland division. He was wounded at the Battle of Guidecourt in which his brother Cecil was killed. Jack returned to the fighting line and won the Military Cross for directing his company in the initial stages of the German offensive in the spring of 1918. According to reports, he and his brother had been the Beau Brummels of St. John's before the war. To use one admirer's words, they were "spatty and glovey" and particularly attractive to women who liked to see men walk "rather than hide themselves behind the wheel of a car."

Mary Quinn and Jack Clift's sister, Flora Campbell, both claim that Jack and Margaret met after the war. Quinn said that the friendship grew into an "understanding", but Flora Campbell doubted this as she indicates:

> Re my brother Jack and Margaret. I imagine they became great friends towards the end of the war in 1918 or even after . . . After his return from the war he went into my father's law firm to study and try to pass exams relating to becoming a lawyer.[3] There was certainly no money being made so marriage was a very remote possibility I should think. As far as I knew there was no engagement.

Campbell admitted, however, that she herself had just returned from boarding school, so that in 1918 and 1919 she "was probably so taken up with her own life that other people's comings and goings didn't register." In any event, Jack Clift died at the age of twenty-six on 12 February 1920 of a kidney disease that was caused by his war experience.

With the alleged tragic romance of a handsome officer and a pretty girl before its eyes, the town of St. John's gloried in weaving apocryphal stories about them. But the truth of the affair lies hidden in the letter edged in black that Margaret wrote to Gladys on the day that Jack Clift died (one of the few letters she ever dated):

> I am so sorry I have not written before, but I have been waiting for this for so long. I don't want to talk about it ever again & please do not mention it. It gives me the feeling of eyes on one's bare heart. Don't let Mother know I cared so much. You see I have not seen him since he was taken sick. I never went to the door to enquire & we only used to write

notes until he got too ill. They say he changed awfully — the illness was very severe. Mother will tell you everything when she goes up. I will be glad for her sake, for she has not been outside the door yet. She had been wonderfully brave but needs a change badly.

I have absolutely nothing to say — I seem to have lost my art with the pen. I hope you are well — you have such happiness in store for you. Don't picture me as a tragic figure — I'm just the same as ever only I can't bear the sight of H.R.B. & H.B. I suppose time heals everything. Forget all about this won't you & be happy as you can. I think those who have gone on are so lucky & happy that it would be cruelty to wish them back. Will write more soon.

Margaret was obviously very shaken by Jack Clift's death, perhaps even to the extent of shying away from the attentions of other men. Although Herbert Robert Brookes and Harry Bell[4] owed her no apology for being alive, one could excuse the girl for resenting their good health and availability, for all of those that she loved best were slipping away: her father had died a month earlier and Great Aunt Chancey was to die a few months later.

Without marriage there was little for a girl of her upbringing to do in St. John's. Although she was intelligent and imaginative beyond the ordinary, nobody had thought of sending her to university. Indeed, she probably did not think of it herself until she felt it was too late. Intellectual privileges were for boys, it was believed at the time, and only for a few at that. The polish of an English boarding school seemed to be all that was required for a person of privilege; but Margaret did not have quite that, although her sojourns in London were enough to make her part of the right set. Mr. Duley's estate, which was worth precisely $49,988.44 provided Margaret and Gladys with $250.00 each a year, a sum substantial enough to enable a girl living at home to dress well and run about with the rich. Bound by the very rigid class system that characterized the isolated, inbred colonial city of St. John's, Margaret made no effort to escape the code of the *beau monde* of the time. Although she did not play golf at the then exclusive Bally Haly Golf and Country Club, nor cut a figure at the Prince's Skating Rink, she did spend a lot of time attending dances and balls which were often private affairs. Many upper-class homes like those on King's Bridge Road and Circular Road were mansions that could accommodate large groups; but for even larger gatherings, the Newfoundland Hotel ballroom was often hired. But the centre of such social activity of the time was Government House, which Margaret frequented so often that she could not bring herself to make fun of its pomposity until she was over forty years old. Similarly, she admired British royalty and often sought out means of associating with it. Among Gladys's notes, for example, is the following: "All preparations & big formal balls etc. had been cancelled by Royal Command & so she never made a début. 1912-13?" These dates are misleading because the mourning period for Edward the Seventh, who died May 1910, was long over and the 1914-1918 war had not yet begun. Gladys's reference to Margaret's début probably means that because of the First World War her sister had missed some sort of ceremonious introduction to Government House in St. John's; but it is possible that the family was contemplating the expensive outfitting of the younger daughter with a train, feathers and long gloves for her to make her debut before the King and Queen at Buckingham Palace. It was the custom up to 1956 for a selection of acceptable young ladies from the colonies, as well as from Britain, to be groomed for this annual event, which gave great satisfaction to the participants and their mothers, and impressed those of the populace who were not Left Wing.

For much of her life Margaret Duley led a double life as socialite and as solitary member of her own private bluestocking society. She ate her breakfast in bed, went shopping, played bridge, travelled, motored around the countryside, took long walks around Rennies River and into the countryside around Smithville "to see daffodil tread down crocus" and "Darwin tulips waving tight secret heads," and went to Government House. Although her name appeared occasionally on the dinner lists, she was more regularly invited to the dances and garden parties. Unmarried women were not often asked to dine in those days. The supper dances were very correct and English with an equal number of single men and women waltzing and foxtrotting in rooms hung with huge portraits of Britain's more recent kings and queens. Even the refreshments emulated English party menus: a typical evening's fare featured sandwiches, two plates of cheese straws, two fruit jellies, two creams, two and a half dozen éclairs, two and a half dozen meringues, two sugar cakes, and shortbreads for twenty couples.[5] The fact that the Duley men were invited for stag evenings of bridge, poker and pool is a clear indication that the family was considered a part of the vice-regal circle in the city.

Since such social activities were not sufficient to sustain her as an intelligent, imaginative person, Margaret read voraciously, joined in the local suffragette movement, and became a member of the Ladies' Reading Room and Current Events Club, which had been founded by Lady Horwood near the turn of the century. At one time, she became Honorary Secretary of this club, which sponsored lectures and offered a reading room with more challenging magazines than the usual women's popular fare of the time. About 1918 the question of women's suffrage and especially the agitation for the granting of the vote to women became a preoccupation with the ladies of the Current Events Club, which had been renamed The Old Colony Club (not the nightclub of the same name). Margaret was one of the leaders of the Women's Suffragette Movement in Newfoundland which demanded not only the parliamentary vote but also the municipal vote for Newfoundland females. As a consequence, in 1920 with the help of W. E. Gosling, the mayor of St. John's, the right to vote in municipal elections was granted to over one thousand women who owned the required amount of property. After this, Margaret and her fellow suffragettes formed the Women's Franchise League, which fought for and won complete enfranchisement when in March 1925 a Suffrage Bill was passed by both the House of Assembly and the Legislative Council. In this way, Margaret helped to make her feminist views a means of political change in Newfoundland that reflected and supported the larger women's movement in Europe and elsewhere. Such activities indicate that Margaret's personality was a dual one. The dichotomy between the outer and inner person, as well as between the thinker and the wanderer, was evident as she played at being a socialite at the same time that she was quietly developing her mind. As early as 1918, for instance, she had been studying the occult and eastern philosophies. As a result, her sister Gladys remarked that when Margaret visited her in Richmond in Virginia around 1918, she had grown "from a very sophisticated young girl to a healthy independent woman eager to read and know all there was to know of the occult and the Past and we had long talks of what she learned of the Psychic powers and self-control of the mind."

Precise details about Margaret's life from 1920 to 1940 are not to be found. In 1928, however, she and Cyril took a trip on the coastal boat, the *SS. Kyle* to Labrador, where she absorbed many of the sights and sounds that she used later in *The Eyes of the Gull* and *Highway to Valour*. Similarly, frequent trips to North Carolina, New York, Montreal, and Toronto became part of an established pattern of travel for her; and in 1935 she visited England, probably to finish and publish *The Eyes of the Gull*. The fact that she did not visit the continent of Europe at this time, in spite of her great vicarious knowledge of its cultures and places, probably attests to the power of the custom whereby travel on the Continent was not the fashion for Newfoundlanders of the thirties. When they crossed the Atlantic, they seldom left Britain; for England was a kind of Mecca to them. Rhodes Scholars went to Oxford and the children of the rich attended English boarding schools; Catholic seminarians and medical students went to Ireland; and a few Catholic children went to school in Belgium and the Grand Duchy of Luxembourg. It was mainly the men in Newfoundland who had seen France, and then only when it was a mess of barbed wire and mud during the Great War. As a result, Margaret did not visit continental Europe until 1953; and, in the meantime, she spent her money in what she called "the fleshpots" of Montreal and New York. She did indulge, however, in a good deal of armchair travel. Mr. Duley had brought a set of books by John L. Stoddard, the American lecturer and traveller.[6] Stoddard was part of what someone called "the education of Everyman"; as such his encyclopedic work contained commentaries, photographs of people, places, architectual wonders, art treasures and paintings from all over the world. As a result, Stoddard's books stimulated Margaret's interest in the fine arts and led her to art galleries and art books; and, indeed, allusions in her novels to great artists like Fra Angelico and Botticelli, as well as to the Impressionist and Cubist movements, suggest more than a superficial interest in painting. Stoddard's books, however, did not hasten her first visit to Europe.

The island of Newfoundland comforted Margaret Duley in summer and staggered her in winter. She knew Conception Bay well, particularly Topsail and Carbonear, the latter providing the setting for her first book, in which the characters were named from her relatives and acquaintances in that seaport town such as Pikes (Pykes in *The Eyes of the Gull),* Wilkeses, Penneys, Tuckers, Coveyducks; Emilys, Dorcases, Mary-Anns, Elfriedas, Josiahs, Seths. Margaret found Calvert and Ferryland particularly attractive. There are pictures of her clambering over the rocks of the Isle of Boys off Ferryland and wading in a small cove there. In addition, she took pleasure in Sunday drives, usually with a party, to various outports where some of the inhabitants opened their comfortable houses to select patrons, served them delicious homemade meals, and sometimes let them have rooms for a brief holiday or a honeymoon. Mrs. John O'Toole, affectionately known as Aunt Agnes O'Toole, catered at her discretion to the chosen, and was well known for her partridge dinners; so that "a bird a man" became her motto. Her fresh stewed rhubarb, thick scalded cream, tea buns and marvellous loaves of bread made her famous on the Southern Shore.

Margaret probably knew Fortune Bay on the Burin Peninsula as her niece Margot Duley Morrow claimed. The Reverend MacDermott, a close family friend, was minister at Pool's Cove, where the Duley boys spent a considerable amount of time. MacDermott recalled Cyril's heroic efforts to reach the remote settlement around 1905, as well as his excitement at joining a venison hunt.[7] Nelson spent some of the happiest days of his unfortunate life there, bagging partridge and rabbits, and doing work around the Williams's houses where he stayed. But there is no evidence, apart from Margot's claim, that Margaret ever made the difficult journey by train and boat with her brothers. As a friend once remarked, she would not have subjected herself to a small steamer that could not provide her with the first class accommodation to which she was accustomed.

The theatre was probably one of Margaret's main diversions, especially since there were good halls in St. John's such as The Casino on Henry Street, which had a fine stage with a proscenium. Local groups presented such operettas as *The Quaker Girl, The Prince of Pilsen, The Geisha,* and *The Belle of Barcelona.* Sir Charles Hutton, a prominent Newfoundland musician who loved Gilbert and Sullivan, offered spirited productions of *H.M.S. Pinafore, Patience, The Sorcerer, The Mikado* and others, with all-boy casts from Mount Cashel Orphanage. In addition, plays were performed by both local groups and by visiting repertory companies such as The Florence Glossop-Harris Company, which came from England in 1926 and again in 1929. Its repertoire ranged from *The Ghost Train* and *Charley's Aunt* to *The Silver Cord* and *Twelfth Night.* The Arlie Marks Players, a Boston Revue Company which was owned by the actress Arlie Marks, visited St. John's in 1925 and 1929. A contemporary programme indicates that this company opened at the Casino on 11 November in "the pseudo-epigrammatic Comedy-drama *That Girl Patsy* and gave the audience their money's worth because as advertised there were "No Waits Between Acts" and special vaudeville attractions were provided "to please the most critical." The Originals, an off-shoot of the Dumb-bells, were also popular in the thirties.

Margaret probably would have preferred to be more intellectually stimu-lated than such diversions could provide for her, for she was outspoken, and had forward ideas; but she lacked the drive to create a less mannered existence for herself. Reverend Butcher said that she certainly felt a lack of mental stimulation: "She was one of the few intellectuals in the small society of culti-vated people in St. John's of those days, but the impression she gave was one of detachment and a feeling of superiority . . . I remember her saying something akin to the fact that it would be expensive and pretentious to start a salon." Butcher felt that she should have been more willing to go out into the life of the town, to mix with the faculty of Memorial University College, and to invite people to her house who were interested in books and dialogues. He was inclined to attribute her frustrations to the "extreme class-consciousness that diminished her imaginatively." Butcher's was an incomplete view because it excluded Margaret's shyness, as well as her fear that her friends would laugh at her if she joined more scholarly groups. She had already experienced derision from her home town when she published *The Eyes of the Gull*. One suspects, therefore, that the air of superiority which she affected was a mask to hide a suppressed sense of inferiority. In addition, it was probably lonely being as talented as she was.

Margaret's shyness was complicated by the urge to attract attention. Several of her close friends told me that she was always acting so that it must have been like watching a stage-performance to see her emerge from an elevator into a hotel lobby. One close friend of hers said that "She would stand stock-still and gaze about her as if to say, Well, here I am. If the Prince of Wales were behind her he would have to walk round her to go on his way." Because she expected a door to be opened for her when men were present she often said, "I always approach a door as if it had no handle."

Consequently, Margaret was sometimes overbearing. One day in 1942, for example, she walked into the Public Library in St. John's and asked if it had any of "AE." The young librarian, who had far more formal education than Margaret, did not know that she was referring to George William Russell, the Irish poet and friend of Yeats and of other writers of the Irish Literary Renaissance. Since the card catalogue did not contain his name under the diphthong, Margaret informed the young woman that he was equal to Shakes-peare, while her tone implied that there was something very wrong with someone who did not know this. The polite librarian kept her patience and eventually found some of Russell's work. Although she laughed when she told the story, she said she never forgot the incident because "Margaret Duley made me feel like two cents." This kind of arrogant flamboyance seems to have been characteristic of the public role that Margaret sometimes played.

Margaret was a handsome woman with piercing brown eyes, shapely legs and figure and lovely dark hair with a touch of white at the widow's peak in later years. She liked deep, rich colours, and was well-known for the elegance of her long velvet or silken housecoats. There was never a hair out of place and to children in particular she always seemed like an actress floating around in flowing dresses, with a cigarette-holder in her hand. The general opinion seems to have been that she showed excellent taste in wearing conservative clothes.

Margaret's fluid and metaphorical conversation was a delight to those who liked her; but to some it seemed too premeditated and rehearsed. One male friend, who enjoyed tàlking to her thought that she was rather like Molly d'Exergillod in Aldous Huxley's *Point Counter Point*, who filled her diary with anecdotes and witticisms for future use and who, her malicious friends said, could be heard reciting her paradoxes in bed before she got up in the morning. It is difficult to say whether Margaret's affectations of speech were contrived or came naturally to her; but it is certain that she enjoyed shocking or perplexing her hearers; one man "looked as shocked as if I had swept the Holy Grail off the mantelpiece." One presumes, therefore, that she probably tested on her friends some of the wonderful allusions that distinguished her writing style such as "You look like Lohengrin loosening the swan's golden chain"; "It was not exactly walking equal like Sheba at the court of King Solomon"; "Like Francesca da Rimini they talked no more"; "Sara felt spacious, like Innocent the Third, Kill them all, the Lord will recognize His own"; ". . . the game is over for her when her Aces and Kings are played. The rest she gets are a surprise"; "English gardens are so mannerly"; or "the Albert Memorial . . . seems a lot of Memorial for one man."

One night in New York, for example, before she was to be interviewed by the media, she was so nervous that she "took two tranquillizers and felt as calm as God." On another occasion when she was asked how she was spending her time, she replied, "I am sticking very close to work and studying French and trying to keep my mind above my belt." She must have floored her gentle brother Cyril, who, when their mother was dying, wondered if it would be all right to go out for a while, by replying sharply that it would be perfectly all right because "Mother wouldn't dream of dying on a Wednesday." In a similar vein, when she was exasperated at people's kowtowing to a handsome, fair-haired member of the Commission of Government[8], she turned to him and asked if it was true that the British Government was built on brawn, not brains.

Another often-repeated story shows her spirit as well as her indignation at slights to Newfoundland. One evening at Government House, as turnip was brought to the dinner table, his Excellency the Governor commented that in England this particular vegetable was given only to cattle. Quick as a flash Margaret sweetly asked her host if he would like some. Although the identity of the man is not certain, it is probable that he was either Sir Humphrey Walwyn, to whom Newfoundland "was merely another ship and the Commission another unruly crew to be whipped into shape by leadership and discipline"[9]; or Sir Gordon Macdonald, who had the sensitivity of a flat iron whenever he gave an opinion or expressed moral indignation. During his vice-regal stewardship from 1946 to 1949, Macdonald served no liquor at Government House and was notorious for making reproving speeches. In one of these he assailed the drinking habits of St. John's by distinguishing between "the beer guzzlers of the west-end and the cocktail-drinkers of the east-end." To be impugned for liking "their drop" did not bother the "west-enders", but to be considered lower in their taste than a rival portion of the citizenry annoyed them. As a result, Sir Gordon was not popular; and Margaret's controlled rebuke expresses her own indignation as well as giving voice to the popular opinion of the Governor of the time.

Beneath Margaret's grand manner and play-acting lay the spontaneity of a child. She loved to dance and often spun round a room for sheer joy. When she had had a couple of drinks, she had an amusing way of doing a little kicking step that delighted her friends. In addition, she was an excellent mimic, and often imitated the Queen accepting a "beah" rug from her Canadian subjects; or Edith Sitwell, with her turbans and giant topaz rings sitting like a great tea cosy reading her poems. She once convulsed a room with her exaggerated recital of Tennyson's "Come into the garden, Maud / For the black bat night has flown" and singing the song "Throw Mother from the train . . . a kiss." She could also give a rousing impersonation of Kitty Wells, the country and western singer. By almost all accounts, therefore, "She was great fun." Although she was aware that she often usurped conversations, she just could not resist taking over when the opportunity arose.

Women generally liked her because they found her a stimulating companion and guest. Those duller or more conventional than herself often had unkind thoughts or perhaps jealous feelings towards her. "Here comes Miss Mag" muttered one; "What a peculiar person," exclaimed another. One woman crossed herself before telling me she disliked her; while another unceremoniously summed her up as "clever, silly, sloppy, romantic, too sentimental and [she] took no active part in things." Sometimes she raised hackles because she flirted with other women's husbands; and at least one person claimed that her men friends usually had "other strings attached to them — legal ones."

To most of her friends in Newfoundland Margaret seems to have revealed little of her inner self. But she was less cautious with those who were not inclined to see her as affected. Ellen Elliott of Macmillans wrote to Marguerite Lovat Dickson, who read for that company during the Second World War, that in all her years in the publishing business she had never met an author who impressed her as much as Margaret Duley: "She is so vital, and alive and so aware with so much of Sheila Mageila[10] and Sara[11] in her own personality. [She has] sophistication plus such frankness and honesty . . . and then the other side of her, [is] so like a brave little girl with a single streak of fear." Mrs. Lovat Dickson agreed: "In all my experience of meeting women novelists (which is slight compared to yours) I have never known one to appeal in such a way. It is so hard to separate her from her work, now — as you say, she is Sheila and Sarah."

29

In this way, Margaret made a lasting impression on people. Marguerite Lovat Dickson wrote to me that Margaret was "one of those rare people who come into your life, not as a stranger but instantly as a friend. [She had] tremendous intellectual vitality . . ." Dickson did not even realize that Margaret was twenty years older than herself. Cutty Kitchell, another of Margaret's friends, said that she was one of those "rare souls you meet on life's path and you're eternally grateful for the light they shed on yours . . ." It is clear, then, that Margaret's personality elicited strong responses that ranged from great admiration to strong dislike.

When they were not intimidated by her intelligence, men liked her. She never tried to be insipidly feminine to attract them, and often scared them off by choosing the witty thrust over the demure smile. Her belief that a woman should have an air of mystery worked as much against her as it did for her, perhaps because few men want to solve a mystery when they meet a woman. The truth is that Margaret's general attitude to men was ambivalent. They could give one babies, companionship, and "the comfort of arms"; yet she was often contemptuous of them. She was such a mixture of the predatory and stand-offish that they were puzzled, and often resented her attempts to analyze them as soon as she met them. As one of her close friends claimed, "She had some very deep and searing love affairs"; but Margaret discussed them so obliquely that one can never be quite sure about either the number or the depth of her attachments.

In addition to men, Margaret also had ambivalent attitudes towards many other things: she both loved and hated Newfoundland; she made fun of the select group to which she belonged but from which she could not divorce herself; she often did not respect Newfoundland's English rulers but liked to associate with them; she believed that her writing was the most important thing in her life yet relinquished it very quickly; she hated being "stripped naked" by publishers but wanted to charm them; and finally, she was repelled by blood but could not resist writing about it.

Any number of reasons may account for her antagonism towards Newfoundland. She was cut off by the island from the cultural activities that she could enjoy in big cities; she was proud of her family's connection with England, and perhaps compared life at home unfavourably with life there. She was often bored; for the social round was not enough to satisfy her. She wanted more freedom for women as much as she hated their economic and imaginative poverty. Consequently, Isabel Pyke in *The Eyes of the Gull* is more than a girl who wants to get away from the rocks and fish offal of her outport home. She is the symbol of hundreds of women who must have chafed against a stereotyped life whether it was lived in the town or the country.

In addition, the First World War had wiped out a generation of young men whose ghosts were never very far away. But above all, the Newfoundland climate exasperated Margaret. Her letters are thus like almanacs in which she praises and deprecates the weather in the same breath: "To-day — outside —

30

nature is putting on a magnificent polar show . . . It has been an epic day. The temperature is five, overblown with a wild North Easter that pounces at the house as if it would gouge it up by the roots. The ground is glassy, the skeleton trees are almost bent to the ground and the hard blue sky is like the glittering eye of the Ancient Mariner." In the next sentence, however, she changes her tune: "when Nfld. lapses into gale force wind and the houses feel porous, and one is sure the wind had to find the bone, displace the marrow and rush through the final passage I feel invaded — and it sounds as if all the witches and broom-sticks were in delirium — but it is a state that is our heritage." Margaret was proud of the beauty of Newfoundland, but also sick of its harshness: "It is a tough country to manifest the perpetual joy advised by St. Paul." As to spring and winter, she writes, "a plague on both these seasons because they are one and the same thing." Once when apologizing to her cousin, Freda Jefferies, for not writing to her, Margaret blamed the weather for her procrastination: "The real reason I am sure, is that like the ruck of my fellow countrymen I have become quite ambitionless due to the complete and utter purgatorial spring that passes for a season." It is perhaps not far-fetched to suggest that Margaret's sensitivity to the unexpected changes in temperature and to the endless months of March and April took the sharp edge off her creativity, and eventually helped her to rationalize her disinclination to write. Being so involved with the climate of Newfoundland, there is little wonder that the crazed winds and the boiling seas are at the core of her most successful books.

When summer came, however, Margaret forgot the exigencies of winter and refreshed herself with the glory of new growth and balmy breezes and the translucent colours of the countryside. Her books thus show the sweet nature of the island as well as its darker moods. Her attitude towards the seasons in Newfoundland reminds one of Thomas Moore's lines, "To love you was pleasant enough/And, Oh! 'tis delicious to hate you."

Margaret's love of children and her desire to influence them suggest that she regretted not having any of her own. Although young people were rather awed by her because she was such a stickler for good manners, they nevertheless enjoyed her company because she did not talk down to them. Her niece Margot and Margot's young friend, Elizabeth Murphy, once good-humouredly endured Aunt Margaret's severe reprimand for their having dared at the age of eleven to sneak on board a foreign trawler in the harbour; neither did they object to being taught to sing "Au Clair de la Lune," or even "Honey Spread on Brown, Brown Bread," the latter to be sung with a great rolling of r's and supper to be pronounced "suppah." Margaret went out of her way to supply treats for her young friends to eat, and at the annual children's Christmas party in the Rennies Mill Road house, she made up wonderful stories and enticed them to play all sorts of interesting games.

Jane Clouston Hutchings and her brother and sister were special protégés of the Duley family after Mrs. Clouston's death. Although Jane remembered affectionately Mrs. Duley's custard icing, Cyril's kind smile, and Nelson's cane, which like Beau Geste's converted into a sword, she said that it was Margaret who had a lasting influence on her. Calling herself "Saturday's Child," Jane ran messages every Saturday for ten cents and gave the cat a bath as well. While "Tabby" was drying before the drawing room fire, Margaret taught Jane a little French, introduced her to classical music on the old victrola, encouraged her to study harder, and promised her a permanent wave if she gave up chewing gum. When Jane suffered from tuberculosis in 1937, "Aunt Margaret" was one of the few who visited her in "the San."[12] In those days, the disease was so prevalent that Newfoundlanders avoided consumptives like the plague. Margaret, sensing the loneliness of the twelve-year-old girl's isolation in the institution, did not make a virtue of avoiding the sick, as others have done, but lightened Jane's burden by taking her for drives and providing various diversions.

Margaret's strongest relationship with a child was with her niece Margot, the daughter of Cyril and Florence Duley. The young girl was fond of her aunt, so that they became good companions, as they talked about books and went for walks which were always a kind of adventure or pilgrimage. Margot remembered being taken to the "Southside" in St. John's, near Riverhead, where Shawnawdithit, the last of the Beothucks, was believed to be buried and where she was given a lecture on the shameful treatment that Margaret believed the native people had received in Newfoundland. Similarly, any monument or statue in the city was the inspiration for one of Margaret's lively commentaries on the merit of service, particularly if the subject was an exemplary woman. She was not, however, sympathetic to children's interest in baseball and cowboys as she wrote Gladys: "All the children here think of nothing but going to Texas, which from the cowboy radio serials and all the horse-heroes, seems to represent a fabulous place where horses run wild and cowboys live like the lone ranger — what a world of radio nonsense we live in — I find the children mentally very trivial — one with a classical mind seems as extinct as the auk's egg." But eight-year-old Margot wanted to go to Texas; so that Margaret as a loving dry nurse was further exasperated. She need not have worried; Margot's mind, "classical" or not, became highly developed so that she is now a professor of Asiatic history in the United States.

As to Margaret's snobbery, it was perhaps difficult not to be a snob in an outpost of empire where upper-class Protestants were considered the most socially acceptable, where only wealthy Catholics who had been educated abroad were permitted to join the charmed circle of high society, and where titles, though few in number, were most prestigious of all. It was characteristic of this milieu that Government House made careful selections of young ladies to dance with the officers from the British warships that steamed into the harbour on courtesy calls, and middle-class children felt privileged when they were occasionally invited to the birthday parties of their betters.

Margaret's niece felt that a lot of her aunt's imperiousness came from the assumption that to be a Duley merited special attention from servants and tradespeople. Other families of the time had the same assumptions about themselves and behaved as condescendingly as she did in the shops on Water Street. "Floor-walkers" were expected to pull out chairs for their customers; clerks were contentedly servile; and everyone knew his place.

Although she drew the line rigidly above and below stairs, and rang the bell from three flights up for service on the dot, Margaret was often kind to the maids. She reinstated one who had had a baby out of wedlock. To another she rented a family house at a nominal amount and would have given her the house except that the co-owner would not agree. She learned to treat faithful Mary Carew more as an equal and asked her to witness her will in 1957 and to testify that the wavering hand writing was hers. It was Mary she wanted to do her hair when she could no longer go out to the hair dresser. As Margaret grew older, she became less exacting about social conventions, perhaps because she realized that Edwardian manners did not suit the atomic age. By 1962 she had long relinquished her reverence for social correctness. Hence, she wrote to Gladys' daughter, Margaret Crowell: "I must also report that I had a good laugh about the woman who is so horrified about candles for luncheon. As you suggested, these are no times for such idiocies. Personally if I wanted to I'd use an old kerosene lamp and then ask Mrs. Astorbilt for lunch. There is no doubt that the old time world is tottering . . ."

In spite of her love of England, she loathed the Commission of Government because she felt it humiliated the proud people of Newfoundland. She was pro-British to the extent that Britain represented the culture and sophistication that she missed at home; but surprisingly she seemed uninterested in British foreign policy as it affected the Third World. When British policy in Newfoundland was in question, however, she was quite vocal about its deficiencies. The Britain of literature, history, tradition was for her peerless; but the Britain of hard-fisted colonialism was anathema. As a result, in *Cold Pastoral* Mary Immaculate writes from London: "I hate to explain myself over here. People seem to be so sure of what should be. Their opinions seem to be polite but seem to be set in cast iron . . . People can be trying, and people are ignorant about the Colonies."

Margaret indulged in palmistry from time to time and even owned a large crystal ball, which sat on the mantel piece in the dining room. Her gazing sessions seem to have been play-acting, as a friend implies: "She had long fingers which turned up at the ends. She would move her hands over the crystal ball to clear it if it had become cloudy. This of course gave her a certain aura." Mary Carew also claimed that there was a crystal ball but that it was kept in the china cabinet. She also said that Margaret sometimes was upset after using it and had to take aspirin and go to bed. Although stories of Margaret's divinations might have been hearsay, her friends never dismissed them entirely. She herself gives a hint about this matter in a letter to Freda Jefferies, who had been in hospital in England: "Somehow I knew all was not well as you know I am a witch about foresight." It seems that Margaret had a kind of second sight, which she may have inherited from her grandmother, Julia Wilkinson Soper. In any case Margaret's "talent" seems to have been put to its most frequent use when she dressed as a gipsy and read palms at charity bazaars as part of her superficial social life.

Margaret's inner life was a different matter. While it would be rash to assume that her wide reading in literature and philosophy narrowed her creativity, it seemed that her knowledge did not meld into a body of thought which would have been seminal to her writing and given it a fully integrated vision. She was so familiar with literature that her novels are embellished with numerous allusions; one has only to glance at the epigraphs to the chapters in her books to realize how much she had read. Having graduated early from Ethel M. Dell and Ruby M. Ayres (whom she hid under the desk at school), she turned to more substantial fare so that she became as familiar with Shakespeare as she was with the Bible. She seems to have been well acquainted with Keats, Shelley, Tennyson and Swinburne. She had probably read D. H. Lawrence's *Lady Chatterley's Lover* because her niece remembered her saying that she had argued publicly against the ban on it. She also had read Lawrence's poetry, as *Novelty on Earth* shows, and she knew something of Aldous Huxley, for she not only owned a copy of *The Perennial Philosophy* but also in *Highway to Valour* Trevor Morgan reads an unspecified Huxley novel during the voyage to Labrador. In addition, Cutty Kitchell claimed that Margaret admired Huxley greatly, while Margaret's inquiry at the St. John's Public Library about "AE." indicates an interest in Anglo-Irish literature, especially since a chapter heading in one of her books contains a line from J. M. Synge's translation of Petrarch.

Margaret's notebooks and marginalia as well as the conversations in *Highway to Valour* show that she had a good working knowledge of French. She owned a French edition of the Bible, read French verse in anthologies, and apparently could also read longer books; in addition, she lent Mary Quinn a biography of Sara Bernhardt in French. At the other end of the scale, she loved detective fiction, particularly the novels of George Simenon, who probably appealed to her because he specialized in the psychology of murder rather than in the bloodletting which sickened her.

The rest of Margaret's reading was philosophical and religious. With the result that her beliefs were as hybrid as her taste in books. Born and bred a Congregationalist, she learned the Bible at her mother's knee. As a young girl she went regularly to church services, and also helped the Ladies' Aid Society at socials and teas. Unlike her parents, however, she did not remain steadfast.

Her presentation of Sheila Mageila, the heroine's mother in **Highway to Valour**, may be partly modelled on Mrs. Duley, and partly on the stern Congregationalists whom she met in St. John's and Carbonear. As a consequence, her book is a repudiation of the sterner side of dissenting religions. Mageila's mother says that dancing is a sin and approves "the minister's sermon about it even when he shook his fists and said he would rather see his children's legs cut off than see them dance." Mageila noticed that the hymns were like jigs, and that the minister "read a dancing psalm, bidding the floods clap their hands and the hills be joyful." Although there was no ban on dancing for the Duleys, Margaret must have found her early training oppressive in many ways. Since euphemisms became a part of her morality, she was perhaps thinking of herself in the scene in which Mageila muses about birth: "Why should a child accept evasions? When she asked her mother what a womb was, she was told it was a word in the Bible. The big red dictionary said it was a place where the young were nourished before birth." Mageila felt Wesley-ridden; Margaret seems to have felt the same way so that she probably began to waver from orthodoxy after she had had a whiff of wider views in England in 1913, later in Canada, and in the United States with Gladys. Mageila's discovery of the beautiful Anglican Cathedral in St. John's seems to confirm that there was not sufficient loveliness or joy for Margaret in her own church:

> . . . she was tired of red plush and the once-a-week smell of the United Church. How to explain to an ardent Methodist that she had found a Gothic cathedral, open all day, where she could sit and see stone so soaring and smooth that it looked like a row of natural arches worn by a soothing sea?[13]

Although she was not bigoted, Margaret seemed averse to orthodoxy and Roman Catholicism did not attract her at all. As a result, in *Cold Pastoral* Mary Immaculate is weaned from praying to St. Joseph, as well as from going to Mass, genuflecting, and eating fish on Fridays. Such practices were considered unsuitable for an outport girl who now belonged to an important family that went to Government House but not to church. Another example of her aversion to orthodox religion is the fact that she was unsympathetic towards the Portuguese fishermen who paraded to the Roman Catholic Cathedral in St. John's with a statue of the Blessed Virgin as a gift. Similarly, there are occasional references in her letters to Catholic customs that annoyed or amused her. Nevertheless it was seen to in the Duley home that the Catholic maids went to Mass every Sunday; and, in addition, Margaret often gave Mary Carew some money for the poor-box or to light a candle for Nelson whose footsteps they imagined they heard after his death; for as Mary said, "I suppose the poor man needs a prayer; he's still on the go."

By 1938 Margaret wanted nothing further to do with organized churches. Although she gave Reverend Butcher the impression of a "pose of superior agnosticism", he felt that it was "a screen for profound sensitiveness, and what I myself would recognize as deep spiritual experience." A Baptist friend from Winston-Salem confirmed that Margaret had a definite belief in God, but it was the God that "she had found for herself", so that much of her religious expression grew out of "the love she had for small things: babies, all small helpless things, dogs, cats."

Cutty Kitchell, who occupied one of Margaret's apartments from 1953 to 1955, claimed that "Margaret was well versed in Kant, Hegel, and Nietzsche" and that she had introduced her to Rudolph Steiner's works. The German mystic's belief that "there is a spiritual world comprehensible to pure thought but accessible only to the highest faculties of mental knowledge" probably appealed to Margaret's interest in abstractions and the occult. She was also very enthusiastic about the American philosopher Joel S. Goldsmith, who was a faith healer and a comforter to those who ask "Why does this have to happen to me?" It is difficult to know how many of his books she read but Mrs. Kitchell said that Margaret carried around two little black books by Goldsmith: *The Infinite Way* and *Spiritual Interpretations of the Bible*. Margaret's copy of the former is well scored, and some of the marginalia are written in French in the wavering hand of the palsied. Christian in emphasis, the book discusses how to achieve hope and peace of mind after Hiroshima. Margaret obviously found it sustaining during the years when she was sick with Parkinson's Disease, but Steiner and Goldsmith had to compete with Annie Besant, Madame Blavatsky and others for her interest.

Margaret was attracted to the Church of Christ, Scientist, when she felt ill and became depressed, as she wrote to Freda Jefferies in the spring of 1954: "I wish you had taken up C. Science — Mentally it is better than even Royal discipline,[14] and though I will never be a professing Scientist I know that the true one is never ill . . . It's all in the Gospels and as the whole ministry was laid on Healing one wonders why the churches have lost it." Almost in the same breath, she tells her to try Steiner because some 'reclaimed' cousins in Cheltenham had discovered him: "I find orthodoxy quite sad as a way of life." Yet unorthodox pursuits led her into a labyrinth of ideas that muddled her thinking, and probably diverted her from her writing.

From telling Freda to try Christian Science, Margaret could turn to advising Gladys how she should conduct her prayer circle: "I have been lucky as I have jumped through all the hoops of the East which from the beginning held the secrets of Release — You must learn to comprehend the Self in man as Knower and which being one with All-Self or Father in Heaven is not born nor does it die — that we only experience through *perishable* personality in order to taste necessary experience — that victory is only in sight when one glimpses no Reality but the All-Self." This kind of inflated terminology lent her the air of a cultist and exasperated her friends. Mary Quinn said that she lost all patience with her because of it: "Before she became so highfalutin with her metaphysical tendencies her letters were a joy — she had a turn of phrase and a humourous outlook that was hers alone, later the letters were full of higher thoughts, mind over matter etc., etc." Alice Sharples Baldwin was also impatient with Margaret's "wholehearted adoption" of "some cult or philosophy which seemed to her to have all the answers," and which threatened to turn her into a bore. Mrs. Baldwin's reference to Margaret's "happy successful period" as distinct from the period of "riding the horse of this later interest "suggests also that her preoccupation with esoteric studies increased after the rejection of her last novel, *Octaves of Dawn*. Meanwhile Margaret sometimes wore "a red shawl to suit the part" and "held forth on these teachings to a group of highly practical, middle-aged businessmen, admirers who obviously had very little idea what she was talking about . . ." To some extent the comments of these two friends throw some light on the unmaking of a novelist. Her friends admitted they never quite knew what Margaret's philosophy was all about. A good deal of it was Eastern. She said that she had "jumped through all the hoops of the East,"and her letters and marginalia include a mixture of Hinduism, Jainism, and Buddhism. According to Gladys, Margaret's interest in Indian philosphy began around 1917: "Margaret studied intensely about Karma and how one must believe one must bear suffering as an honour and never willingly show depression but keep good thoughts forward in your mind as a force in the doctrine of evolution." There is evidence in Gladys's notes not only that Margaret studied Jiddu Krishnamurti and knew his long poem *The Path*, but also that she went to some sort of philosophical school in Toronto. She may even have been associated with a guru at this time. She was certainly very interested in the Hindi *Bhagavad-Gîtá* because her copy has many portions of Krishna's advice on meditation ("fixed upon the Higher Self") heavily underlined and she also used the word "Karma" frequently in her letters.[15] But she kept it out of her novels except for one instance in *Cold Pastoral*.[16]

Margaret also considered reincarnation, but it became only a kind of wishful thinking for her. The very cold January of 1959 in Newfoundland, for example, prompted her to joke to Freda Jefferies in the following terms: "How I would like to re-incarnate on the beach of Wakakii (can't spell it)." On another occasion Margaret said that "Someday perhaps in another age we could continue where we left off." Similarly, towards the end of *Cold Pastoral*, when the heroine decides to marry again, she thinks of her dead husband's love of music with inappropriate whimsy: "In that flash of vanity she was sure Tim's death was the moment for his rebirth. God, she prayed enthusiastically, be kind, and let him be born on a piano-stool."

Whatever Margaret thought about reincarnation she seems to have believed in life after death, at least to the extent of writing some convincing remarks for Sara Colville in *Novelty of Earth*. The very night that Sara was attracted to Murray Blair he shocked her by telling her not to talk rot about meeting her Maker, that there was no hereafter, and that the grave was the end. Her eyes and mouth were "one mystical protest." Realizing that the hallway of Government House was not the place for an argument about immortality, Sara said he was wrong, that the subject was "not a little thing," and resumed her former gaiety. Later, as their relationship deepened, Murray was moved to anger when she insisted that there was more to life than "a sense of direction" and "ordinary decent conduct":

> There's your own entity and what you're made of yourself. You of all people would despise a purposeless life, and all around us is evidence of plan and purpose, letting quiet ordinary people get a glimpse of something infinite. There is survival! We've found something in each other

and strain towards it, and we can strain past it to more absolute beauty. These things can't be without mind and spirit — '[17]

Sara had been equally shocked when Murray had told her that "Christianity was a drug" and that "no Father would give up his Son to save miserable sinners."

Because the nature of Margaret Duley's belief in immortality is indeterminate, she attempted to express it in terms of other writings that range from Hinduism to Walt Whitman, and from Christ to D. H. Lawrence. She once told Cutty Kitchell of a paranormal experience that she had had in which she was engulfed in great blinding white light and seemed to have moved to another plane of spiritual experience. This experience apparently led to her preoccupation in *Novelty on Earth* with Lawrence's poem "Gladness of Death," which seems to indicate that she too believed that after the painful experience of dying, "there comes an after-gladness, a strange joy / and in a great adventure / oh the great adventure of death, where Thomas Cook cannot guide you." References in Margaret's letters to the dying who often "smile estatically [sic] — as if they were meeting their pilot face to face," her words to Freda after Auntie Alice's death, "You wouldn't want to drag her back — & hinder her from going forward," and the passages that she underlined in a Goldsmith chapter "Putting on Immortality" in *The Infinite Way*, point to a preoccupation with the possibility that death was not the end of everything.

In her personal life, therefore, there was something of the mystic about her as she sought by contemplation and self-surrender to obtain absorption into the Deity. She certainly believed in love as spiritual health: "It is like a lovely little hammer that cracks up the hard outer shell." Yet when one reviews her philosophical reading and her letters, her faith appears to be little more than the simple belief that "The Lord is my shepherd; I shall not want."

1. The Elsie books were written by Martha Farquarson Finley, an American novelist and juvenile writer. All twenty books in the series are pious and sentimental; and Elsie herself is a terrible prig. The books sold well up to the Second World War.
2. *Queechy*, (George G. Putnam, New York, 1852). Elizabeth Barrett Browning apparently liked this novel: "*Queechy* is another American novel by a woman, very clever & characteristic." [*Elizabeth Barrett Browning's Letters to Mrs. David Ogilvy*, ed. Peter N. Heydon and Philip Kelley (London, John Murray, 1974), p. 107. Letter dated 9 September 1853.]
3. The practice in Newfoundland was to study privately with a law firm. Attendance at Law School and a law degree are fairly recent requirements.
4. A casual friend, he was an Englishman with the Williams company from Cardiff, a lumber firm that exported pit-props from Labrador to Wales.
5. From Sir Alexander Murray's guest ledger for 1 February 1921, when Margaret Duley was present, accompanied by her brother Capt. Cyril Duley. The governor noted that the evening was "one of the most successful ever."
6. *Lectures*, Complete in Ten Volumes (Chicago and Boston, George L. Shuman and Company MCMXIII), 1897-1898; 5 additional volumes in 1901.

7. *MacDermott of Fortune Bay:* told by Himself (London, Hodder and Stoughton Limited, 1938), pp. 38-41.

8. Government by Commission 1934-1949; three commissioners from Britain and three Newfoundlanders with the Governor as Chairman. It replaced Responsible Government until Confederation with Canada in 1949.

9. S.J.R. Noel, *Politics in Newfoundland* (University of Toronto Press, 1971), pp. 238-41.

10. Apparently in an earlier draft of *Highway to Valour* the heroine, Mageila, is given the double name; later it was transferred to her mother, the daughter retaining the single name Mageila. Nobody could be less like Sheila Mageila than Margaret Duley.

11. Heroine of *Novelty on Earth.*

12. The Sanitorium for lung diseases on the outskirts of St. John's.

13. *Highway to Valour* (Toronto: The Macmillan Company of Canada Limited, at St. Martin's House, 1941), p. 253. All quotations are from this edition.

14. Earlier in the letter she had admired the resilience of the Queen on official tours.

15. The *Bhagavad-Gîtá, The Book of Devotion, Dialogue between Krishna, Lord of Devotion and Arjuna, Prince of India,* from the Sanskrit by William Q. Judge (13 ed., The Theosophy Company, Los Angeles, California, and Theosophy Company, India Ltd., Bombay, India, 1937).

16. (Hutchinson and Company, 1939), p. 177. All quotations are from this edition.

17. Margaret Duley, *Novelty on Earth* (New York, The Macmillan Company, 1942), p. 115. All quotations are from this edition.

CHAPTER THREE

The Eyes of the Gull

Why and when Duley began to write is a mystery. Certainly she was bored; perhaps she wanted to show her mother that even if she could not have a husband and babies she could produce "brain children". The highlights of the Labrador trip were taking shape in her mind; and she was anxious to try her hand at imagery and symbol as her beloved authors did. Perhaps she thought that it would be dramatic for her friends to see her name on a book cover in the show-window of Dicks and Company on Water Street. But she resolved to say nothing until she was in print. This decision continued to be her practice, for her friends said they almost never knew what she was doing until a book suddenly appeared. Sometimes, however, she let intimate friends see part of a manuscript. When she became an author in the thirties, she wrote four successful novels, and then failed with the fifth, the rejection of which so upset her that she did not try again.

It seems that she began, out of the blue, with *The Eyes of the Gull* as is indicated in a letter from the Publicity Department of the Macmillan Company of Canada on 7 May 1942 to Miss Mona Clark, the editor of Gossip Limited, which gives the "low down" on Margaret Duley, while discussing *Novelty on Earth*:

> As a writer, she is apparently a 'natural,' having plunged straight into novel writing without any apprenticeship in journalism or even short story writing as far as I know.

Some months earlier, in the fall of 1941, Duley herself gave the following information to the Macmillan Company in New York, either as an interview for radio, or as some kind of release for publicizing *Highway to Valour*. In this document, the author projects an image of a heroine from an Icelandic saga visiting a softer land. "Newfoundland is a challenge," she announces: "Its sea spits in the face; its wind is like a presence; its rock represents the very hardness of creation; and the weather is like high drama; often like a persecution and then like balm in Gilead." Next Duley switches from her role of stalwart Brunhilde to world-weary modern woman in order to divulge something about the origins of her writing:

> I suppose I am middle-aged (detestable word!) and I have run the gamut of

much living before I tried to write, doing so when I realized I was so very bored with all the Unfinished Symphonies and the same dream with a different face. I wrote secretly and to date I think I have endured all the slings and arrows of outrageous fortune that accompany the effort. I wrote a bad book and tore it up; took another to London and did the rounds sitting like a schoolgirl in front of the publishers.

Nobody knows what the "bad book" was about; but the one she did the rounds with was probably *The Eyes of the Gull*. Mischievously Duley continues by playing up to the interviewers as an unrepentant expatriate who has shed her rough native garb but does not yet know what to wear at Ascot or the Masters:

At this stage of living I have lopped off all the things I fundamentally detest. I did away with scow-like shoes and itchy woollen clothes, and appear in front of horses and on courses in quite the wrong things.

One can imagine the kind of questions that elicited these responses. Canadians and Americans knew practically nothing about Newfoundland in 1941 and it was fun to josh them when they asked whether there were cows and electric lights on the island and "where did you get that nice dress you have on?"

At any rate, the first novel was written because Duley was bored and because she felt she had done enough living to provide her with subject matter. The book was probably finished when she went to England in 1935; so that the writing that Freda Jefferies thought that the author was doing while staying with Aunt Lizzie Martin at Paignton that year was probably revision and proofing. She might, of course, have completed *Cold Pastoral* in England also; but her secrecy about such matters leaves one permanently in the dark.

The Eyes of the Gull was published in 1936 by Arthur Barker Limited in London and received favourable reviews in *The Manchester Guardian*, *The Times Literary Supplement*, *Public Opinion*, *The Observer*, *The Overseas Daily Mail*, *The Yorkshire Herald* and other periodicals. Although the novel was reviewed sympathetically in St. John's, Duley's acquaintances do not seem to have been impressed by the small-town girl making good, as they jeered at her phraseology. Because she made such a small splash in her native waters, there is small wonder that Duley was not yet interested in either an American or a Canadian market.

The setting for this Newfoundland novel probably grew out of Duley's knowledge of Carbonear in Conception Bay, with possibly some recollections of the Isle of Boys, which lies off Ferryland on the Southern Shore of the Avalon Peninsula. The inspiration for the title came from memories of her sea voyage in 1928 as she indicates in an article in *The Atlantic Guardian*, in which she explains why she wrote the book by writing about herself in the third person:

. . . because one summer day, while leaning on the deck of the *S.S. Kyle* in Labrador, a gull hovered in front of her, and she experienced eyes like yellow ice, the symbol of the piteous heart of the north.[1]

Although the Labrador experience was not to mature imaginatively until *Highway to Valour* was written, the dominant images of devouring seas and savage winds were used to good effect in this first of three novels set in "the land God gave to Cain." As a result, it was the Newfoundland background and the uncompromisingly drear finale that received the respectful attention of the reviewers.

The Eyes of the Gull is the story of Isabel Pyke, an outport girl of thirty, who is straining to be free of her bleak life, the rocks, the howling wind, heaving seas, and her overbearing mother. Isabel soon meets Peter Keen, a visiting artist, who leaves her after tutoring her in the ways of love and glamourous living, but who gives her enough money to go to Spain, the land of her dreams. Utterly bereft (Keen's bank-notes are like "oats to a dead horse"), she finally returns to her plans to see Andalusia, only to be thwarted by her mother's sudden paralysis. Isabel courts death, and dies from exposure in a storm. Despite the sentimentality, some banalities of style, and the stereotyped character of the male lead, the book is as hard as a diamond. It is full of memorable people, savagely simple landscape painting, grim humour, the macabre, and a harmonious use of Biblical quotation that achieves choral effects. The chill glitter of the gulls' eyes, symbol of the psyche of the cold "shore," pervades the book and haunts the reader as it does the tormented girl.

The theme of escape is handled skilfully. Isabel wants to go to Andalusia because it represents everything that "Helluland or the Land of the Naked Rocks" is not. Andalusia, however, is not merely a geographic contrast to Helluland. It is the symbol of the universal dream to fly from what is spiritually stifling. Only kind Aunt Dorcas understands that. Isabel's yearning to escape from an island she sees as "savage, bitter, and chill" is not betrayal any more than it is betrayal for Peter Keen to leave England to break from a father whose "mind was set in granite," and who believed that one "didn't show one's feelings much less paint them." Isabel's mother, who is also obtuse, contributes to the emotional and imaginative starvation of the girl, as well as to "her spiritual rebellion to Newfoundland all her life." To emphasize her point that freedom is not necessarily connected with location, the author with a nice touch of irony shows Peter Keen finding inspiration in the very climate that devitalizes Isabel. In both characters there is something of the author herself whose travels gave her respite from a city shabby from rough weather, and which was often bigoted and philistine.

Duley did not either romanticize or distort the outports of Newfoundland in her writing. By not naming the settlement in this novel, she suggests that she wanted to portray country life in Newfoundland as she saw it in more than one place. The Pyke and the Wilkes families were content because they were comfortably off and did not need more than their flower gardens, a drive up the shore, or a local scandal for their imaginative sustenance. Other families who were poor, defeated, ignorant, and slovenly, were unable to scratch a living from rocky soil and uncertain catches. They did not have Seth Wilkes's opportunities.

Isabel was correct when she said that marriage for too many "baygirls" meant having a lot of babies, getting false teeth, becoming fat and ugly, and working from daylight to dark. Marriage meant the same for many town girls too. When Isabel "stared at slatterns in groups of children with smeared mouths" and "looked at the bodies of pregnant woman and back at their joyless faces," there was much of real life in what she saw, just as the odour of male bodies that she notices was typical of many actual men of the time. Few people had indoor plumbing; and bathwater was an extra load dragged from the well and boiled on wood stoves. Pans and jugs became bathtubs and showers. With the side of her that loved Newfoundland, Duley was drawn to the outports; but she was often angered and repelled by the poverty with which the Commission of Government seemed unable to cope except by band-aid measures.

Isabel's sense of isolation is sociologically as well as phychologically true to life. She has no friends; "the girls I went to school with are all married." Many had probably gone into domestic service in St. John's and the larger towns, or, if reasonably well educated, into offices as secretaries or into hospitals to train as nurses. Hundreds, from settlements like Isabel's, were fleeing to the United States, which was viewed by many as the land of opportunity in the twenties and thirties. Men who had many children often left them to find a job in the United States, coming home only once a year to see the latest baby that they had left behind, and to enjoy their warm family life again. Girls went to the States for excitement, or to give their parents one less mouth to feed. Such girls rarely returned except for holidays and showed no inclination to remain. Isabel Pyke typifies, therefore, those girls in Newfoundland who wanted to get away from the fish-flakes and outhouses.

On the whole, then, Duley's view of the outports as presented in her novel is a balanced one. The happiness of Aunt Dorcas and Uncle Seth is real as Isabel's misery. The peacefulness of the landscape, as opposed to the grimness of the elements, is allowed to shine through:

> The sea was even and calm and crept up the beach in a lanquid wash. The boats rested in black bulk and the houses turning every way on the crooked lanes, shone white in the sun. Wood smoke came out of the chimneys in a thin blue, and curled up to a bluer sky.[2]

The gulls are not always screeching, the winds roaring, or the midwife running. Although Duley may not have fully understood outport life with its jollity in the midst of deprivation, her insights are, nevertheless, valid. They may appear shallow in *The Eyes of the Gull* because she was not yet able to create a heroine who could articulate her problems in terms other than of love as in the Song of Songs, and of life as sweet as the orange groves of Seville.

Duley's portrayal of her main characters is very good. If Isabel, the first of her fine-grained outport heroines, lacks the glow of Mary Immaculate in *Cold Pastoral*, and the subtlety of Mageila in *Highway to Valour*; she is, nevertheless, touching in her unappeasable pain, and convincing in her desires. In addition, the economy of her characterization is fitting in so small a book.

On the other hand, Duley's minor figures are splendid. Mrs. Pyke, who has a tongue that would curdle milk, and who is insensitive, grotesque and gluttonous, is forever pontificating, or leaving the print of her teeth in a wedge of cake: "Bella girl, look spry now. Your Aunts are staying to tea. Open a crock of number one preserve, and cut the black fruit cake — the one with ten eggs." Mrs. Pyke keeps a table that would make the eyes of Dickens's Fat Boy glisten. Duley relentlessly characterizes this selfish, opinionated, unlovely woman, as she shows her "distorting her mouth and letting her tongue cleanse the area between her lips and her teeth," and sucking up "a last draught of tea, sweet from the moist remains of three teaspoons of sugar." As she sizes up a nice bit of salt fish to put "in soak", she is shown to be all stomach and no mind; while slave-driving her daughter, she is finally felled, dribbling and gabbling in the grip of apoplexy, one eye shut, the other winking.

Aunt Dorcas is as civil as Mrs. Pyke is churlish. Not unlike the wonderful Mrs. Slater in *Highway to Valour*, and perhaps also modelled on Duley's grandmother, this large-hearted, understanding woman always pours oil on troubled waters. Her Bible in her guide; and she follows it without unction. It is fitting that her comforting presence should fill the final pages of the novel as she urges the searchers towards Head House, while Joe Perry's wagon sags under her immense bulk. She closes Isabel's eye in death, takes her across the beach to lie in her own parlour, and whispers over the coffin, "'Tis just you and me, my maid. They'll never known. You won't go down like Elfrieda . . . The Lord bless you and keep you and cause his face to shine upon you. Rest quiet my maid." Having done all she can, she mails the banknote found near the dying girl to the Chinese Missions, gives a final directive for the comfort of her invalid cousin, and lumbers up the stairs "glad of a rest."

One agrees, therefore, with the critic in *The Yorkshire Herald* who wished that Duley had given us "more of the Uncles and Aunts."[3] But those she has provided are delightful: Aunt Mary Ann Wilkes from Lunenberg in shiny black satin, glass beads and décolletage, daintily sipping her tea, her little finger stuck out from the cup ("Ain't you cold, Mary Ann, with your low dress?" grates Mrs. Pyke); Aunt Susie Cruikshank, tightening her lips when the wine bottle appears, airing her temperance views, and casting a cold eye on card-playing; Uncle Seth, retired sea-farer, sitting with his vest open, blue eyes twinkling, happy with his sealed crocks of Guava jelly, Bay Rum, and dusty bottles of port (reminders of more glamourous days), as he teases Aunt Susie with the Pauline sanction that a little liquor may be taken for the stomach's sake; Uncle Seth fidgeting in church with a posy of boy's love in his lapel, or impenitently unsympathetic to the stricken Emily Pyke who "wouldn't be where she is now if she hadn't been that good to herself, feeding her face from morning to night." It is into Uncle Seth's mouth the author puts the supreme irony of the book: "Poor Bella. It must be sweet to her, her Mother's silence." Even Joe Perry, who drives the rescue wagon, is drawn memorably in clear, simple lines. Reluctant to be out in the storm, scared of his shadow, refusing to go near the house on the Head because he has to stay with his horse, galvanized into carrying blankets by Uncle Seth's bawling at him that he may meet Josiah Pyke's ghost if he stays alone, Joe is as real as a head of cabbage.

Although Josiah Pyke and Elfrieda Tucker are dead, they are ever-present in the book as they haunt the action in a brutal, macabre parallel to the romance of Isabel and Peter. Mrs. Pyke retells with relish the disgrace Elfrieda brings to the shore when she dies of a still-born child by an unknown lover, while her fiancé Josiah Pyke is absent on a long sea-voyage. When Josiah comes home, he digs up her body to look for a keepsake. After building a house on a bare promontory, he disappears, leaving his legend behind him. In her delirium Isabel sees him walking on the Head in his captain's uniform, and tells him the secrets of her heart above the screech of the wind. These two ghostly lovers heighten the contrapuntal effects in the narrative and become the burden, as it were, of a ballad about unquenchable misery.

Only Peter Keen[4] weakens this strong band of characters, for he is a soap opera Lothario who preaches threadbare maxims about love, freedom, beauty, and who, as he says himself, muddles the values of an inexperienced girl. Despite his terrible dream, he picks up his easel and his Liebfraumlich, and departs, accompanied by his butler. For a brief moment guilt makes him hesitate: "Sometimes when she left him, Peter Keen stared moodily at the sea. Some of his serene sureness in the mutability of things dropped away, and his zest for change lost its edge. A germ of humility crept into his heart and he didn't know what to do with it." True to his conviction that "There's always change: new scenes, new people, new contacts, and the best is only a fugitive thing", Peter bestows his benediction of the banknotes on Isabel, and catches the train believing that she will keep her promise to him to go to Spain. Although he has too much to say in a novel in which the author could have allowed the more interesting characters greater scope, Keen is useful in helping Duley to create tragedy, and to reinforce her theme that the imagination must not wither through the interference of narrow-minded people. As with all Duley's male "leads", Peter is given no quarter; hence he is made to look small. He could have decided to take Isabel with him and then been thwarted by Mrs. Pyke's illness and by Isabel's decision to stay with her mother. The stark, controlled ending of the book could have been retained, and Peter could have gone without shame. As commonplace as he is, one feels that Peter has been victimized by his creator.

The weakest parts of the book are the meetings between the lovers. In these places the dialogue exhales a thick fog of amatory clichés and hyperbole: for example, "He kissed her untouched mouth, silky with olive oil and virginity"; "Within myself I feel as if I could take my feelings for you to the feet of God"; and finally, "You're so sheer. I'm not worth all that." Equally fatuous is Duley's emphasis on the heroine's fineness of feeling, especially in view of the numerous times she peels turnips, draws chicken, and kneads bread-dough. Words like virginal, undefiled beauty and golden skin are used continually; while Peter prefaces almost every sentence with the vocative Isabel. In one chapter alone he uses the name fifty-seven times, and throughout the novel about one hundred and seventy-five times. As a consequence, Duleys' style always becomes banal when the two are together. In addition, Peter Keen's response to Isabel's body is expressed in curious terms: "She had a way of lifting it out of her waist and pointing her breasts to the wind that maddened him with its beauty of line." With perhaps some justification, Duley's so-called friends laughed uproariously over this image. They did not acknowledge, however, the book's tight structure, acute characterization and the primitive force of its Newfoundland setting. Having noted her own amusement, Duleys' friend Mary Quinn gives an assessment of the response to the book in Newfoundland.

> However, my serious reaction is that on the part of Margaret from the grave I'd thumb my nose at them. They tore her apart when she was alive, held her books up to ridicule — at least her first one and the only thing they could find in *The Eyes of the Gull* was 'she pointed her breasts to the wind' and made it the subject of derisive laughter.

Had they read more carefully, they would have been aware of Duley's understanding of line and colour and her skill with spectral themes, as well as her spare style which suits very well the book's atmosphere of desolation.

The macabre tale of Elfrieda and Josiah, for example, is handled masterfully:

> He dug her up to see if there was any token in her coffin; and when he didn't find one he shook the dead thing until her head cracked against the ice. 'Twas a moonlight night, and a couple that was living close by, saw him clear as day. They were afraid to go out; he sounded that wild, but they waited until he was gone and then went across the graves and found the dead creature with her face turned up to the sky and her shoulders froze to the ground.[5]

Very fine also are Duleys' descriptions of storms as the wind, for example, whirls the soggy green banknotes among rocks and brush to fly free, only to "catch and stick again," on their way to the white-capped sea. Striking also are the sensuous landscapes of light and dark that evoke Duleys' fascination with the spirit of Newfoundland's coast.

The gulls provide the central, expanding image in the novel. Snowy-breasted but sinister, the birds symbolize the ferocity of Helluland and the psychological hazards of escape, as well as the cruelties of Fate. Whenever they swoop through the air and Isabel's eyes encounter theirs, she cannot visualize Spain. Even though they presage her death, Peter Keen ignores their warnings. One flies past his face in his nightmarish vision of Elfrieda Tucker lying beside her empty coffin as her upturned eyes seem to become the eyes of Isabel Pyke. Peter is afraid of another seagull which he had painted into his portrait of Isabel and which had terrified her: "He hadn't been able to show the eyes of the gull, but their yellow ferocity had gone into the slightly curved beak." The painting "had seemed to run away with him and paint itself." The look of death about it scared Isabel because its "touch of dissolution" reminded her of a picture in the family Bible of Lazarus looking "black and hollow and decayed around the eyes" as he emerged from the tomb: "Don't I look a little bit like that? . . . [Isabel asks]. I do Peter, and also like the people I've seen in their coffins only my eyes are open."

As omens of evil, these birds dominate the tragic aspects of the book. They are implicit in the graveyard scene as the heartbroken girl sobs over the weather-beaten tombstone of Elfrieda Tucker. They are not far from Mrs. Pyke's bedroom where her winking eye stares terribly at her daughter as if it were proclaiming the mother's longevity; and they are near the minister as he prays with unconscious irony for grace to enable Isabel to bear her affliction with "meekness, humility and sweet submission" to the will of God, as well as for Mrs. Pyke "to give thanks for the ministrations of a kind and loving daughter."

In addition, Isabel is aware that the birds are near "in the night by the black stove" when she contemplates matricide and suicide: "the other alternative she dared not name — she seemed to meet a continual closing door. she might have known! It was the meaning of her last look into the pitiless eyes of the gull."

Sometimes Duley softens her style to catalogue lovingly the flowers in an outport garden, or to describe lilacs round a door, or "the vagrant waddle of fat geese in blocks"; but more often her words are bald to suit the eerie power of the story. While the humourous and pretty touches are perhaps fitting, it is Duley's depiction of a formidable land, crazed lovers and gothic atmosphere that makes the book memorable. As the events move to their relentless close, one feels something like the cathartic effect of a Greek tragedy. Stern and uncompromising, *The Eyes of the Gull* is a striking first novel. As the London *Observer* said: "There is no elaboration or waste; even in her defects the author shows an admirable firmness."[6]

1. "Glimpses into Local Literature" (July 1956), p. 26.
2. *The Eyes of the Gull* (London, Arthur Barker Ltd., 1936), p. 58. All quotations are from this edition.
3. (19 November 1936), p. 3.
4. A possible prototype of Peter is Rockwell Kent, the American artist who painted in Brigus during First World War. He, with his family, was deported as a suspected German spy. See Patrick O'Flaherty, *The Rock Observed* (University of Toronto Press, 1979), p. 132, Note 26. See also Kent's autobiography, *It's Me O Lord* (New York, Dodd, Mead & Co., 1955), p. 280, for possible prototype of Head House.
5. p. 21.
6. (15 November 1936), p. 188.

CHAPTER FOUR

Cold Pastoral

Margaret Duley's second novel, *Cold Pastoral*, is also set in Newfoundland. It was published in London by Hutchinson and Company almost certainly in 1939, although it is undated. There is a fifty-two page publisher's catalogue appended to the book. Since the inclusion of such advertisements was not very common after 1915, this advertisement makes the first edition of *Cold Pastoral* of some interest to the literary historian and professional bibliographer as well as to the reading public. In this publisher's list, Duley's book appears under Love and Romance on page sixteen where it is praised as a "strange fantasy of Mary Immaculate born among the fisherfolk of Newfoundland . . . a most entrancing story." On the back of the dust wrapper, the book is described as a "pure romance [which is] told with great charm and understanding; its strange heroine has a sweet and simple quality that is most refreshing." This was probably the only critical attention that the book received in England because it was not reviewed by the papers that had covered *The Eyes of the Gull*. One assumes that the publishers were probably unable to promote it, since Hutchinson and Company was bombed early in the war, and all their records destroyed; hence, it seems unlikely that Duley made any money from the book.

Duley's declaration that the characters "are entirely imaginary, and have no connection with any people or particular place in Newfoundland" is misleading. The truth is that the story was suggested by the mishap of Lucy Harris, a little girl from New Melbourne, Trinity Bay, who was lost in the woods for eleven days in March 1936. Lucy survived her ordeal, but her frostbitten legs had to be amputated. In addition to this story, *Cold Pastoral* is a version of the rags-to-riches motif, which has the double setting of town and country. Mary Immaculate Keilly, an outport girl of thirteen, loses her way in the forest, is found and taken to hospital in St. John's. Mary never returns home because she is adopted by Philip Fitz Henry, the doctor who saves her legs. As Mary grows up with his aristocratic family, Philip falls in love with her; but he is unaware that for four years she has been having an innocent romance with Tim Vincent, the boy next door. Betrayed by Hannah, the jealous housekeeper, and shattered by Philip's accusations, the young people elope. Married and confused, they quarrel. Tim rushes off and dies after a car crash; and Mary goes to England to recover from shock. She decides not to finish her university education and pursues instead a more conventional life by marrying Philip. This tale would be hackneyed indeed if it were not for distinctive characterization, good dialogue, the Newfoundland setting, and some lyrical writing in the early part of the book.

Mary Immaculate and Josephine, her mother, are the most striking characters in the book. Mary is an unusual girl, for she dislikes the beach, the stage-head, and cods with slit bellies; and prefers instead "the new green of the junipers and the white pear-blossom drifting uphill." She is a kind of nymph who was born on the sea because her mother ventured forth too late in her pregnancy. Later she becomes a beautiful toy to her rough, insensitive brothers and to her parents who do not know what to make of her. Religious, superstitious, innocent, kind, free-spirited, mischievous and intuitive, she is an enchanting child who continually defeats her mother with questions: "What was the sky made of? Was it solid enough to hold the feet of God and his holy angels? If it wasn't, why didn't they fall down in the valley? Did God lie on his stomach and look down? . . . Was the devil rich enough to buy coal for hell-fire, or did he stack up a woodpile like themselves? How much kindling would it take to burn a lost soul?" Mary's fantasy, however, is equalled by her candour as Josephine indicates.

"Mary, tell the good Father who made you."

"Pop," replied her daughter with cold finality.[1]

There are other delights to be found in this child who believes in "the Little People" and who, having deliberately kicked over a fairy-cap, lies cowering in bed for fear of being "held"; who gives the "changeling" Molly Conway a bouquet of wild flowers because everyone shuns her; and who coaxes a holiday from school on a glorious day of silver-thaw. In addition, Mary dares to omit "the ceremony at the door," that is, blessing herself, and genuflecting to the statue or oleograph of the Sacred Heart and the little lamp on the home-made altar, before she leaves the house and dances into the crystal forest singing, "I've got sin on my soul, I've lied as big as a dog. I'll go and burn in hell fire. The devil's got horns and a tail. The fairies have little wings. Who'll choose, who'll choose? Left hand, right hand . . ." Mary is also quick-witted in handling a snobbish town girl: "'My mother wouldn't let me invite you to my house." "No," said Mary Immaculate gently; "Lady Fitz Henry wouldn't let me go. She wants me to have nice things in my life." Mary's hanging narcissistically over the studio photographs to be sent to her mother is memorable: "Philip, I'm lovely." Likewise, one remembers her near drowning as a nonswimmer as she insists that she wants to go "forward in that long lovely way" because she thinks she can do it like other people. As ethereal as thistledown, Mary is also as substantial as her burly brothers. Only she has the courage to drown the wounded bird and to frighten Hannah with the fate of Humperdinck's witch; or the malice to ask Philip for money for an abortion for her friend Maxine, even though she knows full well that he will think it is for herself. This fascinating girl, who looks like "gardenias on ice," who sticks a geranium in the hand of the marble angel above Mater's grave, who helps a cat cross the street in London traffic, and to whom a river is an endless source of enchantment, is never wearisome. Even her town language and her cove language are alternated effectively. When Lady Fitz Henry is dying, Mary prays "from some savage memory of the Cove": "God spare her the death-rattle."

Josephine Keilly fortifies the structure of the novel against its splintering into too many fragments of whimsy. Although Duley repesents her realistically with cavities in her front teeth and the smell of dishwater and cooking clinging to her clothes, she becomes something of an anagogic figure. As such, she is the similitude of the Newfoundland fisherman's wife who is his equal on the fish-flake and in the storeloft, as well as in managing the kitchen and the vegetable-patch and in teaching children their prayers. In addition, she shows independence by coming to town, heedless of Benedict, on "my own bit of money from the few eggs I sold." In turn, she is unselfconscious and unenvious when she meets Mary: "'My!' she breathed on a long exhale, 'ain't you grand now, Mary Immaculate! Let me look at you! You've grown like a weed and no mistake! The like of it, in a real silk dress and not cut from a remnant I'll be bound.'" After examining her daughter's bloomers and petticoat, she turns towards the Fitz Henrys, more at ease than they are, to discuss baits and traps with the great fish exporter's widow. There is no condescension in the author's admiration for the fisherwife's fine qualities: "In Benedict's world a woman could make or break a man. Had he been bound to a slattern the toil of her hands would have been for naught. Josephine made him!" Josephine helped "make" Mary too because she had the imagination to let the girl go free to revel in the beauty of the outdoors. One of the most poignant moments in the book occurs when Josephine rises from the crunching snow as Mary is carried away: "The distance between herself and her daughter was widening, and she could not catch up. Hurrying as fast as her legs would permit she could only keep her in sight." One wonders whether Julia Soper of Carbonear felt the same sense of loss when her child, Tryphena, went to the wealthy Chanceys in St. John's to become their adopted daughter.

Apart from Mary Immaculate, the main characters are somewhat disappointing. Lady Fitz Henry is a stereotype of the patrician woman; Philip is the servant of the plot as noble physician, prig, and jealous lover. David Fitz Henry is more interesting than his brother probably because he is not the traditional male lead who is rarely successful in any of Duley's novels. Felice, David's wife, is merely a nice girl. Tim Vincent, sharing the limelight with Philip, is certainly not dull, but he sags under the weight of the roles assigned to him by the novelist, for he suffers from the author's insistence that a boy of fifteen is not a hobbledehoy but a prodigy of highly developed sensibilities with unerring taste in books and music, as well as a flair for acting out the parts in *The Book of Operas*. In order to satisfy Duley's appetite for metaphors Tim plays in turn Hansel, Tristan, Romeo, Glaucus, Browning's Pied Piper, and Kipling's Lew of "The Drums of the Fore and Aft." At the age of twenty, he takes on the traits of frustrated lover, pianist and discontented engineer. Even the author herself seems to doubt his verisimilitude when she has him ask Mary Immaculate if other boys and girls behave as they do.

Duley's ancillary characters are excellent because she gives them that touch of ghoulish humour which is a distinctive feature of all her novels. There is Benedict Keilly, trying to get his wife, who is in labour, and his skiff home in a squall, bawling at her not to put a haunt on the boat, to pull herself together and not to "go dying" without a priest to bless her, or gloomily shaking his head over Teresa, his son's consumptive wife, and foretelling that Dalmatius "won't get the winter out of her." There is Molly Conway, with her frightful expanse of bare scalp "pink and pitted wrinkled like a prune," her hands venturing to touch Mary Immaculate's golden hair, or walking "like a scow lying back on its keel" as she leads the searchers to the lost child; and the sour busybody Mrs. Houlihan, whose skin is "as grey and as mottled as the belly of a cod;" as well as Mrs. Rolls and Mrs. Costello intoning, with relish and inaccurate memories of the Royal Reader, "And the sweet face of Lucy Grey nevermore was seen", while Mrs. Houlihan snaps that she "don't hold with poultry," and "'Tis not Lucy Grey they're searching for, Mrs. Rolls, and I never heard of no moor in these parts."

The servants in the town mansion are adequately characterized but do not compare to the originality of the women in "the Cove." There is Hannah, who is "rancid," "mildewed," like "mouldy sails," as well as nasty and jealous of Mary. Hannah is a convincing Mother Holle, who is finally defeated by her own warped nature. There is also Lilas, who joins the Salvation Army after she is jilted and takes to teetotalism and testifying. When she marries a policeman, she discards her bonnet and pours his drinks with a loving look. Her sense of delicacy will not permit Mr. Philip to deliver her babies, because she has passed him so many dishes at table. It is interesting to note that Lilas's chatter about conjugal bliss seemed to give rise to the gossip that the author used to tell her friends that they had not lived if they had not slept with a policeman. Duley writes in *Cold Pastoral* that "Mary Immacualte was interested to hear she would not know she lived until she slept with a policeman." It seems that contemporary gossipers used this statement by Lilas as if Duley had said it of herself.

The quality of *Cold Pastoral* is damaged when Duley takes her heroine out of "the Cove" on page fifty-two of her three hundred and thirty-six page book to expose her to the ceremonies of upper-class town life. If the narrative had ended with the rescue, it would have been a pure idyll; instead, it is adulterated by too much whimsy and prosaic romance.

The book is faultless when it treats the seasons, the sky, the sea, silver thaw, and the lore of a people living on rocky land hemmed in by beaches that are strewn with caplin spawn. Although all three Newfoundland novels give details of the diet, occupations, pastimes and superstitions of the outports, *Cold Pastoral* deals most extensively with folklore. Belief in "the little people" permeates the life of "the Cove"; and Mary Immaculate never really rejects fairies. In the book men, women and children fear being "held"; Uncle Rich for example, finds his way out of the woods only by turning his coat inside out, and making the sign of the Cross. Likewise, Benedict Keilly, when shooting partridge in October, is "taken," and walks all night in sight of his campfire without advancing a step until he remembers to bless himself. At other times a piece of bread is the charm to placate malevolent fairies. Molly Conway, the deaf mute, is considered a changeling because a cousin wheeled her out one day without putting a crust in the baby carriage. Religion is no bar to superstition in the novel. Mary Immacualte's misadventure is blamed on her failure to genuflect to the home-made Sacred Heart altar in the kitchen; but her recovery is attributed to the piece of bread in her pocket. A "settin'" of eggs offered to St. Anthony will find either lost objects or lost people without any reference to bread or the sign of the Cross. Contradictory beliefs never worry the people of "the Cove", for they also have their home-made cures: foxgloves for heart trouble, crackerberry leaves for indigestion, coltsfoot for consumption, live trout let up and down the throat for whooping cough, and an axe under the bed of a woman in labour to cut the pains in two.

Once the story moves away from this kind of atmosphere to the more artificial life of St. John's and London, the lyric quality associated with white pear-blossom drifting uphill and chill snow disappears. The fine texture of pastoral is thickened by a ferment of sensational incidents and literary allusions. Nothing that follows the episodes in "the Cove" equals the precision with which Duley's paints landscape in the early part of the book:

> The sea was different from the land! There romance ended and realism began. Where cliffs dropped in sheer descent, challenge roared at their granite base. From the flat meadows above, an occasional sheep dropped to death, remaining impaled on jagged rocks until the sea sucked it strongly to itself. On still days venturesome children lay on their stomachs, staring down with ghoulish eyes. The green waves playing over the woolly heap held them with a strange attraction. They couldn't know it was there and not look! One memorable day a cow dropped over. It was heavy and gave the sea stronger work. Green and blue, grey-green with seaweed brown, colour changing, fading, leadening it all washed over the red and white cow . . .
>
> Over the hills and away from the sound of the sea the fairies seemed friendly and real. There were many places for them! Secret little groves where the sun shone through in golden chinks, wayward marshes threatening to the feet, and many ponds blowing with sedge and purple weeds. Others were completely covered with heart-shaped lily-pads and white and yellow flowers dreaming in the sun . . .
>
> The wood-pile was a stack of glass spruce. Glazed sawdust by the

wood-horse made a pool of yellow on the ground. A bit of wire netting
had become a frosted cobweb . . .
The sea was blue and far away, while on the land stood forests and
forests of crystal trees. Running into them she sped through endless
trunks. Sometimes the sun came through and made golden spots on the
snow. Even the shadows were full of light, and where the junipers bent
and met a slim spruce they made a glittering arch. Deeper and deeper
she ran into the crystal forests.[2]

Duley's experimentation with imagery and symbol is not entirely successful
because it makes a mishmash of what one may call "a medley of purloined
conceits." The title *Cold Pastoral*, which is taken from the final stanza of Keat's
"Ode On A Grecian Urn," is relevant largely as an affirmation of the quality of
the scenes in "the Cove" where "a glass world shining in the moonlight" and
cold beauty of March in a Newfoundland outport create poetic effects. The
emasculated epigraph on the title page (". . . maidens overwrought, with forest
branches and the trodden weeds — cold pastoral!") is unlike the epigraphs and
titles of Duley's other novels because it seems to have little relation to the point
of view of this book. Since Keats's vision of life and of the permanence of art is
not integrated into the story, one may assume that Duley's use of his poem is an
example of the many unassimilated literary allusions used to make Mary
Immaculate unusual.

Some of the references are apt though whimsical. Hansel and Gretel,
together with Tristan and Isolde, represent the double relationship of Tim and
Mary as one of childlike romance on the one hand and awakening passion on
the other. The white sails on the ivory ship that Tim gives Mary are a perfect
symbol of their innocent and ill-starred love, just as black sails are an apt
illustration of Hannah's mean nature. Unfortunately, Duley is not satisfied
with merely transposing Grimm's fairy tale and Humperdinck's opera and
running them parallel to Wagner's *Tristan and Isolde*. She also multiplies allusions until the reader is surfeited with German opera and quotations from
English poetry. Even "Les Noyades", Swinburne's brutally sexual ballad about
a pair drowned in Carrrier's purges during the French Revolution, is inap-
propriately attached to the romance of Mary and Tim. Eventually even the
Tristan-Isolde comparison breaks down because Philip Fitz Henry, who plays
Mark to Tim's Vincent's Tristan, does not lose his bride.

The possibilities of this trio effectively representing the recurring theme of
love as the marriage of two souls undivided by death ("Don't they live on in you
— us — because it is we who will carry them around . . . I don't need to go to
Tim's grave to be with him.") are destroyed by Tim's lachrymose deathbed
scene and by the metamorphosis of Mary Immaculate into a society girl who
chooses the soft life, as well as by general overwriting. At times, Duley does not
seem to know when she has said enough.

A great relief from literary references is the presentation of upper-class St.
John's in the thirties. Having become a Fitz Henry, Mary Immaculate is reared
in a hot-house atmosphere of proper accents and proper manners. She is de

Romanized in spite of Josephine's determination that she would not sign away her rights to her daughter unless she were reared a Catholic. But the Fitz Henrys break faith: "Mary can go to Mass. Any bias will be mitigated by other associations," Mater told Philip. Because so few Catholics were considered the "right" people at the time, the child was sent to a snobbish little school, "standing in a square of trees," where "daughters were sacrosanct from the rough and tumble of larger schools," and where she is a "bay-noddy" to her choicer class-mates. This school is probably modelled on Rockford, a small, non denominational, private school in St. John's that received its impetus from parents who were convinced that their children would receive a better educa- tion in uncrowded classes. A headmistress, Miss Glover, was imported from England to oversee her staff of one. As a result, a one-room school was opened in 1929 in the Missionary Hall of the United Church on Queen's Road, across from Long's Hill, where a patch of green turf and some trees lent something of the air of an ornamental garden to a gravelly city street. The pupils, both boys and girls, wore English public school uniforms; and, in Duley's novel, Mary Immaculate's uniform differed only in colour from those worn at Rockford.

This educational haven for the élite was an important part of the social history of St. John's, expecially as it illustrates the background of class distinc- tion against which Duley sets her characters. Rockford prospered until 1937 when Miss Glover decided to sell it. She allegedly sealed a bargain with a Miss Phillips in England, who decided to take it after seeing some photographs of part of the church and the tiny park to the west with its few shrubs and flowers. Miss Glover, probably without malice, had distinctly given the impression that Rockford was set in grounds like those of an English estate. Miss Phillips was elated and soon set sail for Newfoundland. On board ship she met the Re- verend Jacob Brinton, a clergyman from St. John's, whom she told of her good luck in owning the only school in Newfoundland "for the sons and daughters of gentlemen." Amused at her pretensions, Brinton informed her that his sons and daughters were the children of a gentleman, and that they did not go to Rockford. Not much abashed, Miss Phillip's euphoria collapsed only when she saw her school, which was surrounded by tall, wooden, box-shaped houses standing on unfenced, dusty gravel, and bordering the lip of another hill up which red tram-cars squealed and scraped, and actually stopped beside her door. The story goes that she took Miss Glover to court, and received some compensation. Her plans, however, petered out in a couple of years, and the pupils were dispersed among denominational schools. Gradually, the Rockford refugees settled into the routine of more cross-grained establish- ments while waiting to be sent abroad to be polished up.

In *Cold Pastoral* Mary Immaculate is not encouraged to make friends even at school; she is barely allowed out of sight. She and the boy next door meet in the garden in a tree into which he pipes her with a tin whistle, and they become fast friends. She needs his music, his youth and his chatter to fortify her against the exacting, though kind, regime of an aristocratic household; and he needs her to make him forget his uncle, "a regular home Hitler," who plans his life while the boy's ineffectual mother looks on.

The social criticism in the book is equivocal. Duley sometimes seems to survey the Fitz Henrys with an ironic eye, for they are modelled on the well-bred people who came to Newfoundland from England in the eighteenth century to establish themselves as mercantile princes. The "codfish aristocracy", as they were sometimes called, brought with them their French-polished furniture, Persian carpets and educated accents. They reproduced in Newfoundland an English class system that was joined by those Newfoundlanders who had gone to boarding school, who knew how to decant port and sherry, and who were determined to be English in their manners.

When Mary Immaculate asks her nurse if Philip is "the man with the barracks and the mother that's a Lady instead of a woman," there is more than the innocence of a "bay-noddy" in the question. Later she learns the importance of Government House as she asks: "Why does Mater go to this and nowhere else?" David tells her that "Mater was brought up in a tradition that considers an invitation like this a command." The Fitz Henrys were on the dinner list and were well aware that to "merely attend the receptions and the garden parties was socially second class."

It is also clear that Duley had misgivings about the exclusiveness of Mary Immaculate's upbringing. Her graduation ceremony at Memorial University College shows the Fitz Henrys to be aliens in their own home town, who know nothing of an institution founded in honour of the sons they and others had lost on the battlefields of France and Gallipoli. When Mary should be dancing the night away with the students, she is having a pineapple soda with David, Felice, and Philip because she has no friends. David makes an effort to point out that Mary "needs to rub shoulder with her own age and to raise merry hell with the half-love of calf-love"; but any serious reflection on the class system is cut short by an ultra-smart remark about lesbianism as David and Felice wonder who sent Mary her one gift of flowers.[3] Unaware of the middle class, they would never think of the boy next door.

Thus Duley's awareness of the dangers of social insularity is reflected in her novel. Although she appears to blame the Fitz Henrys for Mary's crisis and Tim's death, her condemnation of their life-style is implicit rather than explicit. In spite of the ironic tone of the book from time to time, there is a general acceptance of their self-esteem and their customs. Although the terms "Mater" and "Pater" were not unknown appellations among a few families in St. John's in the thirties, they were more usually found in imported Christmas books like *The Greyfriars Holiday Annual for Boys and Girls*, or in Lord Peter Wimsey's paraliterate patter. An outport child, even one as finely spun as Mary Immaculate, would have giggled into her cupped hands because she was incapable of calling Lady Fitz Henry "Mater".

As the novel progresses, Mary reflects even more ambivalence in the author's attitude to class. The reader is bothered by the fact that the girl never visits her family. In London she is told of her mother's death by Philip, who assures her that he has sent flowers. Mary's only response is, "She was such a good woman", after which she asks him to tea the next day. Earlier, even Philip had wondered why Mary had shed her past so completely. His mother's response is not persuasive: "Natural enough I think. It's sentimental to cling to places where there is little harmony." The reader is not convinced by Mary's fleeting memories of home, or by her amused reflection on Philip's solemn wish that she be buried in the same plot with the Fitz Henrys: "If she lived long enough the fisherman's daughter would begin to feel dynastic . . . Was she in such a plight that she should be clubbed with some great kinsman's bone?" Duley's declaration that the new Mary will reflect all her life "the antecedent compassions and realities of her origins" does not ring true. One feels, therefore, that Mary lets the reader down. Among snobbish groups in St. John's "an increasing knowledge of cliques made her treasure Tim as a classless boy," yet when Mary thought of the bay, she remembered her father's "inarticulate grunts," his "clod-hoppering into the kitchen" and her never having seen him kiss her mother. In the latter part of the book, the once enchanting heroine has become conventional. David Fitz Henry is wrong when he tells Felice that Mary is "not the type to be cloistered," for she wilfully shut herself into a society that she had led the reader to believe was suspect.

Duley's attitude to killing, although she dwells less on it than on the class system, is, nevertheless, more consistently stated in the book. War is a curse, Duley believes," and David Fitz Henry, who is badly wounded at Beaumont Hamel, where his two brothers were killed, becomes spokesman for the author: "I see nothing in war to recommend it and my mind seethes with heresies"; and he claims that a "gentleman is not supposed to show his feelings. They beat it into you at school and then send you out with bayonets." David wants to give his medals to the charwoman's boy to play with because to him being a hero means "returning without Arthur and John" and being responsible "for Father's premature death," as well as eating bully beef while others are being blown to bits: "I'm against war and I don't care who knows it, and they're going to have it again, Mary, and all for naught." Felice's wish for a world where "a cat, a dog and a bird can lie down with the lion and the lamb" is passionately repeated in her next two books, so that it is clear that Duley loathed killing and bloodletting. Hence, in *Cold Pastoral*, David hates the annual Newfoundland sealhunt: "The killing of the seals distressed him and when one of his father's captains told him they wept real tears, he no longer went to the wharves when the laden ships came in."

Towards the end of *Cold Pastoral* abortion is briefly debated when Maxine asks Mary Immaculate for money to terminate her pregnancy and Mary is revolted by the request:

' Maxine' she accused, 'what you plan is murder!' . . .
'Rubbish! It's absurd! Murder for something that's barely started?'

'It's life,' said Mary Immaculate inflexibily.

Mary also believes that it is an insult to ask a doctor to perform the operation; and she capitulates only when she wonders ". . . what man can visualize the special agony of a woman outside convention?" Since Duley does not broach the subject again in her books, it is impossible to know her full views. This incident is merely an appendage to the plot of the novel to allow Mary Immaculate a modicum of revenge against Philip who, having once already insulted her chastity, will now think that the money he gives her is for an abortion for herself. The whole incident misses fire as an extension of the heroine's character because the author confuses the details. Near the end of the novel the reader is told that Mary Immaculate "coldly . . . entertained a thin steak of cruelty running like steel through her veins. Some new attribute in herself demanded recognition, and she saw it as the capacity to hurt someone, deeply important." Five pages later, when she asks Philip for sixty pounds, she is appalled at her own stupidity: "So sure of her chastity she had not contemplated he might think it was her abortion." As if one about-turn is not enough, Mary makes a second on the very next page, when she admits she *did* think of punishing him by deliberately misleading him about the baby. This seems to be rather too much for good measure because a whole moral issue is clouded by the exigencies of a love story that the author ends in reconciliation. It should not have been introduced a dozen pages from the end of the novel.

In a word, *Cold Pastoral* is an uneven book because it tries to do too much. Its structure suffers from the lack of proportion between the space given "the Cove" and St. John's. The attempt to bridge the gap by having Josephine come once to town to see Mary Immaculate, and by scattering letters from Josephine throughout the book, does not work. The triple setting, the inconsistencies in the characterization of Mary Immaculate, the plethora of literary allusions and the multiplication of melodramatic events, lack the cogency and single impact of *The Eyes of the Gull*. Isabel Pyke's vision of life does not waver for she hates the shore; but in *Cold Pastoral* Mary prevaricates.

When the scene shifts to St. John's, the story loses its immediacy because the author dallies too long with the conventions of the "silver fork" school of fiction instead of bringing to life the oldest city in North America, as she had "the Cove." In fact, London, as portrayed in Mary's letters, has a much stronger reality than St. John's. Glimpses of the old-world town, with its unique harbour, steep hills, cobble-stone streets, bull's-eye shops, and newsboys in tweed caps yelling "Telack-grr-iam" "(*Evening Telegram*), and side-sleighs with passengers muffled in beaver rugs, never appear in the novel. One feels that the novel would be much better if such scenes were included in it rather than so many of the biscuit-tin scenes of Mary waltzing with Philip on the moonlit family skating-rink, or dipping her hands in the coloured reflections from the Christmas tree on the lawn. Brief references to the Cathedral of St. John the Baptist and to "Provehito in Altum", the motto of Memorial University College, are about all the flavour of St. John's that one may find in the novel.

Perhaps because of these weaknesses, the book made no impression on Canadian publishers. The Ryerson Press "slumbered and slept" over it and Macmillans refused it even though Ellen Elliott thought it was beautiful and could not understand why it did not do better in Canada. Her approval, however, carried little weight with publishers and Duley had to rest content with praise from Leo Cox, English born poet and friend of E. J. Pratt, who told her that anyone who created Mary Immaculate must be worth knowing better, "and that [she] had written of background with real power and as that is a masculine subject he is confounded at a woman doing it."

1. *Cold Pastoral* (Hutchinson and Company, London, 1939) p. 18. All quotations are from this edition.
2. *Ibid.*, pp. 7, 22, 33, 38.
3. *Ibid*, p. 237.

CHAPTER FIVE

Highway to Valour

Since *Highway to Valour* is Duley's best book, it seems appropriate to devote some space to her relationship with its publisher, the Macmillan Company of England, especially since it was her first experience of publishing a novel on this side of the Atlantic. In October 1940 she wrote to G. E. Rogers of the Canadian branch of Macmillan that although the Leland Hayward agency was working for her in New York she was, nevertheless,

> very desirous of achieving the Canadian market. The times are sadly out of joint in England and other than that this side has more comprehension of less civilized backgrounds — & Nfld. is a country very close to the bone. America appeals to me with its deeper drop of naturalism. I would come to Toronto if you like the novel — I love it myself but not fatuously.[1]

She said much the same thing in her interview with Macmillan's Publicity Department in New York in the fall of 1941, and added "that a book written on this side should be published on this side." Anxious to have her novel published for her own gratification, Duley, nevertheless, wanted it to be a bell-wether for Newfoundland writers as well. In mid-December 1940 she wrote to Ellen Elliott: "One of the things regarding a Newfoundland novel is that there are no writers from this country and I feel we must emerge sometime and nothing could be more auspicious than the enormous influx of Canadians into my country."[2] War seemed to have made the time ripe for Canada to become aware of a novelist from a little-known island off its east coast.

About the time of her mother's death on 16 November 1940, Margaret sent *Highway to Valour* to Macmillan; and fearful of rejection, she wrote them on 19 November not to return the manuscript, for she would pick it up herself later. She need not have worried because the readers at Macmillan were impressed. Ellen Elliott and Marguerite Lovat Dickson were enthusiastic in spite of their reservations about the last chapters. Elliott, for example, tried without success to persuade the author to delete the scene in which a veterinarian chloroforms two old cats and a kitten. Although she felt that the death of Brin the dog and his burial in the garden had been masterfully handled, Elliott found the episode of the cats revolting for reasons she could not fathom. She also believed that the last three chapters were a striving after effect in style, that the reader was more conscious of words and phrases than of the story, and, moreover, that the war background was not presented clearly and sharply enough.

Duley's reactions to this criticism ranged from good humour to irritation and heated self-defence. She expressed all of these responses in a letter which Ellen Elliott received on 27 December 1940:

> I cannot tell you how widely I smiled over your repulsion of the cats — !
> It is always that way, I find — So many Gods — so many creeds — a
> dog-mind and a cat-mind — I might delete the cats for you — & cause a
> pang to those who worship these gorgeous egotists — of whom I am one
> — I adore the fatuity of the dog — but my cats keep me in the sight of my
> size.

The tone of this letter increases in its pitch as Duley writes that she has been through the suggested revisions twice and was perplexed by them: ". . . with them came so many angles that the integrity of the writer ceased to count — I was avid to co-operate at first & then bewildered by so many minds." Because she was recovering from flu and feeling sorry for herself, Duley next described for Ellen Elliott the terrible condition in which the book had been written as a defence of its integrity.

> I am tempted to say this, Miss Elliott, even while realizing your experi-
> ence & the sensitivity of your ear to MSS — I cannot think I was striving
> for effect in my last chapters — Actually *Highway to Valour* was written
> under intolerable circumstances — my mother dying horribly, my
> brother was a self-destroying invalid & I was a death-devoted vessel —
> That is why I wrote the book — to stay sane — It was written with great
> sincerity & though I know I am too florid with words those are my
> inborn faults — which I do not seem able to master.

Realizing she was probably over-reacting, Duley finished her letter by further insisting that there was no affectation in her book (she was living too close to the bone for that) by offering to weed out any repetitions that the readers found tedious. Ellen Elliott realized that Duley was nervous and tense because the publishers had not yet committed themselves to a contract, that her mother's death had unsettled her, and that the point about striving for effect had hurt her. Hence, in an answering letter, she explained that she had not meant to upset the author and claimed that the cats did not repel her because she was a "dog person," but because she felt the artistic effect of the death of Brin was injured by what had to happen to the cats. She thus advised the author to leave the book alone for a while, and then look at it with fresh eyes.

Since the manuscript of *Highway to Valour* is not to be found, it is hard to say whether Duley made any alterations to the book. The cats remained, and their disposal is so convincingly and promptly treated that one wonders why it was a bone of contention in the first place. Perhaps she shortened the episode. Whatever she did, the final version is completely in harmony with the attendant events and with Mageila's sensitive character.

Meanwhile, negotiations concerning publication continued. A copy of the manuscript was also in New York, and Duley waited and wondered if she should visit Macmillan. Although she was understandably impatient, matters moved quickly; so that the book was out in less than a year after she had submitted the manuscript. It was March 1941, however, before the terms of a contract were mentioned. These discussions continued until June, by which time Duley's mind must have been reeling from the complexities of the publishing experience in North America. She was then in Montreal "working herself up in a state of nerves, doubt, and despair", according to Mrs. Lovat Dickson. The publishing policy of the Company seems to have puzzled the author. In the forties all books in Canada were published either in the United States or Great Britain. Thus to capture the Canadian as well as the American market, Duley had to send her script to New York, where it was handled by an agency, Leland Hayward Incorporated. Frances Pyndyck of that Madison Avenue firm undertook to deal with the American branch of Macmillan concerning *Highway to Valour*, and a little later *Novelty on Earth*. After it was agreed to publish both books, a supply of them was sent to Toronto to be stamped with the imprint of the Canadian Macmillan. During this time, Miss Pyndyck, Ellen Elliott and Duley engaged in a long correspondence about the labyrinthine ways of agents and publishers. From the tart remarks in Ellen Elliott's letters to Duley, there seems to have been no love lost between her and Frances Pyndyck because Elliott obviously begrudged "those slimy toads down there" (i.e. Miss Pyndyck and her associates) the ten percent commission the author would have to pay the agency.

The whole business had a touch of high comedy about it. While the splenetic Miss Elliott was urging Duley to accept the contract that the New York company offered her because publication in the United States would serve the author's best interests, Pyndyck was gravely wondering if Duley was English or Canadian. It seems that her nationality had to be established before an American contract could be drawn up. Since Duley did not answer Pyndyck's insistent enquiries, Ellen Elliott answered for her with restrained irony towards this ill-informed Yankee:

> Since Newfoundland is a Crown Colony, I think Miss Duley would be regarded as English. She certainly is not Canadian. I imagine any Newfoundlander would be disgusted to know she is regarded as either English or Canadian or anything other than a Newfoundlander. They are an independent breed, you know.

On 4 June 1941, however, all Duley's worries about proofs, dust jackets, blurbs, terms, and family interference ended when the American and Canadian contracts were signed; and on 10 July Ellen Elliott wrote to her: "I think Macmillans in New York have started to set — which is always a bit exciting, isn't it?" By August the author was enquiring about presentation copies, and was advised by her hard-headed mentor that she could have six copies but not to give them away to her friends — "let them jolly well buy them."

Duley's contract with the publisher provided to the author $250 at its signing and $250 upon publication of the book; in addition, she was to receive 10% of the retail price of each book sold. The Canadian edition sold for $2.75 and the American one for $2.50. *Highway to Valour* came out on 23 September 1941; by 15 October four hundred copies had been sold; and, in addition, Ellen Elliott reported that Macmillan hoped to sell a thousand by Christmas. Since Ellen Elliott had earlier written that "very few novels sell more than five hundred," Duley's book was clearly very successful.

Both at home and abroad the book was received with enthusiasm. The *Star Weekly* in Toronto wanted it for newspaper serialization; Metheun in England brought it out in 1943 in a small edition to conform with wartime economy standards; and it was displayed on book stalls in British railway stations. In addition, T. J. Wheeler of the Wheeler Newspaper and Magazine Syndicate thought that it would make a good film with Barbara Stanwyck as Mageila. The reviews were plentiful and largely approving. The *Globe and Mail* thought it offered "an exceptional picture of life in Newfoundland and Labrador" and carped only at the author's error that Canada declared war on Germany on 12 September 1939, whereas it was actually 10 September.[3] *The New York Times* praised its "word gift," its "strange glamour" and the rightness of the ending which was worthy of a book that made no compromises with inner reality.[4] *The Saturday Review of Literature* was impressed by its imagery and poetic prose.[5] *The Toronto Daily Star* heard in it "the same dark tones, the same breath from another world that fill the music of Sibelius with the peculiar magic of the North;"[6] and *Saturday Night* saw the book as a novel of "unusual merit".[7] Duley was very pleased with such responses; but she was also tickled and "overcome by things reviewers weave round one — I am now searching my soul for my Sibelius touch — but so far — it belongs entirely to *The Toronto Star*."

It seems that few people read the book with indifference; and there were some, of course, who sounded a sour note. The reviewer for one American newspaper, for example, after praising the landscape painting and characterization, balked at the second half of the novel because it descended to a conventional level by putting Mageila "as a French governess in a melodramatic household . . . [so that] Mageila of the sea-sigh name seems to lose part of her magic."[8] Richard Mohr, in another unidentified review, thought that the novel had "a large amount of overworked pathos, too much talk and too little action."

J. R. MacGillivray's assessment of Canadian fiction for 1941 contains some interesting remarks about *Highway to Valour*. Although MacGillivray thinks the book worthy of "mention", he misinterprets it by seeing the heroine "as a tense moon-struck Newfoundland girl" who "has magic powers of healing and recoils in trembling distaste from life as she meets it in Newfoundland, Labrador and Montreal."[9] There is no "skimble-skamble stuff" about the horrific reality of the 1929 tidal wave, and Mageila does not recoil in distaste from life in Newfoundland as MacGillivray claims; on the contrary, she commits herself to nursing on the harsh Labrador coast.

Like Duley's two earlier novels, *Highway to Valour* is set in Newfoundland; but in addition it is dedicated to the island which, she confesses in her foreword, she both loves and hates. The title of the book is a translation from Ovid's line "A highway is made to Valour through disasters." The story is based on the actual earthquake and tidal wave that occurred on the Burin Peninsula on the South Coast of Newfoundland in November 1929. Late in the afternoon of 18 November an earthquake shook the area and reverberated throughout the island; but it was brief and people thought the danger was over. Around 8:00 p.m., however, a tidal wave struck, which gouged cliffs, eroded the seabed and smashed houses and boats. Twenty-seven people were killed and many injured. Medical supplies, nurses and doctors arrived on the *S.S. Meigle* on 21 November. It was stark tragedy for those who lost families, homes, and the boats which were their livelihood.

Although there is no evidence that Duley went to the South Coast to see the effects of the disaster for herself, she could get a good idea of events from the newspapers and from Mr. MacDermott, who was pastor in Pool's Cove at the time, for he would have been among those who helped out while the battered communities waited for the supply ships to arrive. In addition, her brother Cyril would have kept her up to date because he was privy to detailed information as a member of the Executive Committee of St. John's citizens which was organized to aid the various districts. As the Chairman of the Outport Contact Committee, Cyril probably engaged his sister to be part of the proposed ladies' auxiliary. Margaret was certainly awed by the immensity of the occurrence as she explained in the aforementioned release given to Macmillan's Publicity Department in 1941:

> With regard to *Highway to Valour,* there are more things in heaven and earth and Newfoundland is full of them. I met a strange little boy who was the seventh son of a seventh son and he had the gift of healing in his hands. This gave me the essence for the girl, Sheila Mageila,[10] but the leitmotif of the book is the *sea*; passing through the waters and not being drowned as it were. There was a tidal wave in Newfoundland, following a general earthquake shock, and while I was experiencing the latter I was humbled to a standstill by the realization of man's utter helplessness in the face of natural forces. I asked myself as the house shivered, why man bothered to fashion weapons to destroy himself when nature could do it for him? Then I thought of man's God-given brain capitulating to the high immorality of making machines of destruction instead of machines for the aid and *use* of man. By these devious pathways I wrote *Highway to Valour.*

Duley's treatment of these materials is compact; she does not separate the quake and the tidal wave by several hours but allows them to follow each other immediately. Choosing carefully from the reports[11] and dovetailing them, she dramatizes the horrible scene as houses are swept out to sea in the brief, poignant account of the Michelet home. She bases the death of Sheila Mageila and her daughters on two separate losses; in the first incident, Mr. Thomas

Fudge of Port au Bras saw his house being whirled away, together with his wife and three daughters in it. All the boats having been destroyed, Fudge ran a mile to Bull's Cove but he was too late to effect a rescue. Similarly, in Duley's novel, Pierre Michelet is drowned in an attempt to rescue his family. Likewise, in a second incident at Port au Bras also, another house floated away with a woman inside standing at the window and screaming to attract attention. She too was swallowed up by the sea. In the annals of the calamity at Burin this victim was known as "The Woman at the Window." Since Duley's grandfather had been a fisherman and her uncle George William Soper owned a barquentine, the Duley family had close connections with the sea; consequently, tales of disasters and premonitions were part of her childhood. Duley was aware of the effects of such influences in the writing of *Highway to Valour* as she notes in the foreward to the novel:

> The author of this book wishes to say there was an earthquake and tidal wave in November, 1929. Though this event devastated a whole coast she has used neither time nor place, nor any special fatality associated with the tragedy. The idea for the book is entirely her own; and where it suited her purpose she devastated a whole settlement, calling it by the imaginary name of Feather-the-Nest. All other Newfoundland names are authentic except Ship-Haven and this was invented also, for fear Newfoundlanders might feel compelled to seek identifications. The Irish Princess, Sheila Mageila, is romance rather than fact, but the author knows that some of her own relatives claim her as an ancestress. Other than that she has no knowledge of authentic descent, so she felt quite free to found the family of Dilkes in Ship-Haven . . .

The defensive tone of this explanation of her sources is more than obviated by the authenticity and power of the account of the disaster in the novel. The story of Sheila NaGeira Pike, "the Carbonear Princess," has been part of the oral folklore of the Avalon Peninsula for over two hundred years.[12] Duley's connections with that seaport town enabled her to hear many versions of the adventures of the beautiful daughter of a seventeenth-century Irish king. It was said that John Pike, a handsome English pirate, captured her, ceased marauding, reformed, married her in France, and brought her to Newfoundland. They first settled in Bristol's Hope, and then in Carbonear, where she was revered by the community for her charm and her miraculous powers with the sick. In Rodney Soper's garden in Carbonear, there is a long slab of stone that was said to cover the resting place of John Pike and his royal Irish bride. The tenuous relationship of the Duleys with Celtic sovereignty probably came from the marriage of Mrs. Duley's sister, Mary Ann Soper, to Segar Pike, or from the alliance of Captain George William Soper, Duley's uncle, with Emily Olivia Pike, or perhaps from similar connections among Carbonear Sopers, Pikes, and Wilkinsons.

Duley made double use of this legend by giving Sheila Mageila, the heroine's mother, the courage and leadership of the Irish princess, while reserving her beauty, charm, and gentle powers with the sick for Mageila.

Sheila Mageila made such capital out of her ancestress that "power was intensified in [her] and advantages hers by the right of the Princess . . . She accomplished the unusual through her own exalted infallibility." Mageila was lovely, gentle, and contemplative. Sheila Mageila's name, as the author said, "retained the lustre of Deirdre in the Ulster cycle of Ireland." The inhabitants of Feather-the-Nest respected Sheila Mageila; indeed, they loved her youngest daughter.

As a consequence, *Highway to Valour* is the story of the effect of the tidal wave on Mageila Michelet, a sensitive girl from an outport that is "pinched between land and sea." Orphaned by the disaster, Mageila goes on a boat trip to Labrador with her grandfather, meets Trevor Morgan, who is English, married and a civil servant in the Commission of Government. They fall in love. But Trevor soon continues the journey north; while Mageila goes to St. John's where she becomes the privileged French governess in an upper-class household. When the lovers meet again their happiness is short-lived because Trevor's wife refuses to divorce him; and, as a result, he leaves for England to fight in the Second World War. Mageila goes back to Labrador to nurse and to use her power for healing. Although Trevor and Mageila may meet again, they are still apart at the end of the novel; and by concluding in this way Duley underscores her persistent belief throughout the book that "the meeting place of friends is in the heart."

The book begins on a wintry afternoon when Mageila walks across the settlement to cure Bertie Butler's toothache. "First snow is delicate," she thinks: [It is] "soft as a chick, white as a duck on a pond, different altogether from the dense piling up of drifts." Yet the splendid afternoon cannot take away her feeling of foreboding that "the world was holding its breath for deep reasons of its own" and that "Christmas would not come." These early scenes establish not only Mageila's sensitivity to nature, but also Duley's power to mythicize a time and a place. Her lyrical prose engraves the physical surface of Newfoundland on the mind of the reader:

> There were so few people around that she walked alone, coldly bathed in the dwindling glare of the western sky. Marvelling again at the stillness, she savoured the relaxation of a Newfoundlander perpetually tightened from the torment of wind. Now she felt herself walking softly like an Indian, moccasin-clad, easy in body, unblown and unpuckered. Occasionally she paused, knowing she was seeing stark beauty bathed in red. A streak of sunset on snow made her think of blood on white fleece. Her narrow world had brought her close to the slaying-knife, the axe, and the barbed hook striking at the fruit of the sea. Blood, blood, she thought unhappily, visualizing the beauty of the slain lamb and the proud strut of the rooster laid low on the block; but she bade herself look at them, knowing such things must be.[13]

Blood is one of the dominant images in the book; and like the cruel sea, it becomes a symbol of Nature's dichotomies. In this passage, it is glorious in the fierce purple of a November sunset, repulsive on the fleece of an innocent lamb, and beautiful in its implications of the slain Lamb of God. Because Duley knows that terrible things often happen, *Highway to Valour* becomes her declaration of faith, as well as Mageila's, in the face of life's inscrutabilities.

At the Butlers', Mageila cures Bertie's toothache by "going round the pain with quiet circular motions"; and later she is having a cup of tea when the earthquake strikes. After the crash of crockery and furniture, there is complete silence until Mrs. Butler begins to moan about her dishes, and implores Mageila not to leave her. Frantic to go home and certain that the demonic ocean is holding something terrible in reserve, Mageila nevertheless makes more tea, and then turns to leave. At the door she stops dead in her tracks as she sees a solid wall of water moving up from the beach as the tidal wave hurls itself forward. In a moment the Butlers' house slides out into the heaving harbour and is washed in again. Mageila is safe but all her family has perished; as a consequence she must live with the terrifying image of the keels of ships sliding over their bodies.

The description of the disaster is a remarkable piece of writing. Although nothing is omitted, there is no self-indulgence in words as the inexorable truth is told. As a result, the reader is as stricken as Mageila as she watches her home drifting out to sea and realizes that there are no boats to go after it:

> Her eyes become nailed, feeling they must crucify on Feather-Cake with its points leaning for a last look at the land. Frantically she knew her mother stood in a window like a stony figure weighted on either side by her sisters, but in spite of her dreadful maternity she bent towards the sea
>
> 'Papa,' she beseeched, 'what will I do? Where are you?'[14]

The atmosphere of horror as everything was humbled by the sea is evoked masterfully: "There was no need of a cemetery with no one to bury . . . those high up on the hill had climbed higher to look down on those who sat on their roofs . . . she saw a group of sheep with spindle-legs extended in the air: Sheep cannot turn over, said her mind to her hands . . ."

Almost willed back to life by the strong faith of Mrs. Slater, Mageila waits for her grandfather Dilke to arrive by steamer; and he later takes her to Ship-Haven, the world of the Dilkes, where her mother's sisters, all house-proud and marriage-proud, are big fish in a small pool. Mageila almost seems to smother in the close atmosphere of "good cups," crochet patterns, three kinds of sandwiches and Methodist hymns of the Dilke home, until Captain Dilke seeks a cure for her inertia and fainting spells by taking her on a sea voyage to Labrador.

In the novel, the ship, the *Assou* (Beothuck for sea-gull), is modelled on the *Kyle*, a coastal steamer and mercy ship which, from the end of May to early December, brought supplies and mail to the Eskimos and settlers in Labrador, and which, homeward bound to St. John's, brought hospital cases back to North West River, Cartwright, and St. Anthony — a round trip which took from eighteen days to three weeks.[15] Usually about forty cabin passengers were on board the *Kyle*; indeed, as indicated earlier, Duley herself made such a voyage in 1928; and there is no doubt that she drew heavily upon this experience for atmosphere and minor characters in *Highway to Valour*. Although she does not catalogue the names of many places, and does not make much of the stopover at the Grenfell Mission settlement in St. Anthony, she nevertheless evokes the "sufferment" of the sick who live in a wind-bitten land without enough doctors and nurses.

There is little doubt that Duley experienced some of the things she describes in the novel. About two hours out of St. Anthony, one of her companions rested himself unwittingly on a coffin as Trevor does, only to jump off quickly at the rough laugh of a passing steward: "'Hi, Mister! You're sittin' on a stiff. We're taking him home in salt.'" During her voyage, she may have heard the district nurse being questioned by inquisitive Americans, who were horrified by tales of operations performed by the light of a kerosene lamp, as well as of dog-teams labouring through blizzards to a doctor with sick people strapped to the sleds behind them and of babies being delivered on grubby newspapers. Icebergs, huskies, winches and ropes, freight hauled on board, whales, blubber, offal on oily water, the sealers' toast "Bloody decks," the fogs that "came and went like restless ghosts, but when they settled . . . merged into one grey presence," and the beauty of the Northern Lights streaking through the midnight sky harmonize on such a voyage into what may be called a full epic of Labrador. But Duley makes very little use of such details in writing her novel. Most readers would perhaps like a closer acquaintance with the people and their way of life than Duley provides, especially since she saw the inhabitants swarming onboard the *Kyle* at the various stops to gossip and hear all the news. She did note three of the crew rowing the mail ashore,[16] but she did not seem to notice that they delivered it to the last and farthest house which always doubled for a post office in the community because the distance allowed the visitors on the ship a longer time to hob-nob.[17] A gaggle of women and a pack of men on the deck or in their front yards would have heightened the already intensely graphic quality of the writing in her novel. Although the *Assou* went as far north as the Eskimo part of Turnavick and called at Makkovik and Ailik on the way, Duley did not seem particularly interested in describing the native people or their culture. Instead, she was content to use such materials in her short stories rather than in *Highway to Valour*. As a result, the scene in the novel at the oldest Moravian Mission in Labrador does not seem sympathetic:

> They learned the history of the Moravian Church in Labrador, of the Brethren settling far away to divert the Eskimo from his plundering ways. From the deck of the ship they first saw the short squat men with their broad Mongolian faces seeming like a design for lustreless passivity. They saw them stand like stout human pillars until they swarmed towards the *Assou* in dories and kayaks.[18]

Duley even refers to one of the women as "a jabbering old crone," and allows Trevor to suggest to Dr. Britten that he "try another squaw" for his photograph; but Britten likes the one he has picked: "She's so toothless and weather-beaten. I want to get every wrinkle." Although the ugly old woman, the flies, "her small hovel" and the mission-lady's one sad primrose are undoubtedly accurately recalled from Duley's own experience, this scene is unsettlingly dispassionate and fastidious.

Mageila Michelet, the heroine, is in part modelled on "the strange little boy" mentioned earlier, the seventh son of the seventh son who had the gift of healing in his hands. Similarly, as "Good clean Newfoundland stock crossed with French blood," Mageila is the seventh daughter of a seventh daughter whose power to drive away pain earns her the sobriquet "little doctor". Compassionate, intense, sheer like chiffon, she blends with the mists, the grey seas and the pale sunshine of Newfoundland. After the tidal wave, she is like a displaced mermaid who belongs neither to sea nor land. As such, Mageila's task is to learn not to flinch at life's barbarities. As an unusual girl, who is much like the author herself, she is familiar with and loves Shakespeare and the Bible. In addition, in her grandfather's house in Ship-Haven, she reads the Brontës, Charles Darwin, Thomas Huxley, George Eliot and John Henry Newman. Renan's *Vie de Jésus* with its denial of miracles and its scepticism about the divinity of Christ makes her feel less oppressed by the shadow of Sheila Mageila's Methodism:

> Because of the overemphasis of church in her life, she gripped something that took Jesus away from the Wesleys. Though she read beyond her she recognized the reverent presentation of a very human Jesus; and when she came to the crucifixion she was so moved she wept bitterly, seeing Him as *taken* in death as the stags and as unconsoled as her own people . . . How explain she was weeping for Jesus? How make them understand the book made her ponder on the miracles and spend hours watching the sea? Did He make the tempest obey His will? Could He have calmed the tidal wave? If storm was the other half of calm He would be in both, and He would not go against Himself.[19]

Like the novelist also, Mageila is a born thinker and a mystic, if not in the tradition of the saints, at least of those who apprehend truths beyond the comprehension of ordinary people and who surrender to something within them that is bigger than self. As such, she is no ordinary girl as she ponders

> the way she felt when she charmed away pain. Inwardly she explained it to herself. The sun was round; the moon was round; the earth was round; the sky was round above her head; her hand felt round over the pain and her flesh felt part of the flesh she touched. She had a sense of the unbroken circle, of lines that must not be jagged and sharp in spite of the daggerlike rocks rising from the sea.[20]

During her sojourn in Ship-Haven, Mageila is an enigma to her aunts, whose blunted sensibilities will not permit them to understand anyone who plays the piano, listens to the opera every Saturday afternoon on radio, and has no interest in a hope-chest, nor any ambition to marry a bank clerk who may one day become a bank manager. Unbeknownst to her aunts, therefore, her acute awareness of the problem of suffering permeates her nature. For her the interlocked antlers of the stags' heads in her grandfather's house are the emblems of pitiless nature; hence she faints when she hears that they were found in Labrador locked together. "Poor things, poor things!" she whispers. "Don't mind! Don't mind! Humans go like you did, just as hard, just as wild." Blood defeats her; so that she faints again when her Aunt Molly serves roasted bullock's heart for dinner; and it is not until she endures the whaling scene in Labrador that she knows she has achieved greater control of herself and can therefore accept that storm is the other half of calm and that God would be in both: "and He would not go against himself."

As such a perceptive girl, Mageila is a rare mixture of innocence and wisdom: "She had no coquetry. She did not mind a long silence. Quite sub-feminine indeed." Whether she is eating ice-cream, chatting casually with shipboard acquaintances, or singing a rousing song in the saloon of the *Assou*, there is always a disquieting gravity about her. The reader is thus acutely aware of "her nun's" eyes as if fixed on another world and of her sombre response as she remembers "that silver sea leadened, evergreen blackened." Soft smiles but little laughter light up her face; and her reflections are never superficial. As she carries to his master's door the old dog Brin, "whose bones gave no heat," her thoughts turn to the Old Testament:

> Gave no heat? Her Bible-training stirred, presenting old King David, stricken in years, with no heat in his body though they covered him with clothes. Abishag, the virgin, had lain on his bosom to keep him warm. It was all right she supposed, thinking of love seeking no identity. Then she frowned from the feeling of sad old bones in her arms. It seemed more natural for David to accept his age without the warmth of Abishag. She could not have liked cheating nature.[21]

This passage reveals not only Duley's skill with Biblical allusion but also Mageila's contemplative nature. Whatever the angle from which one views this lovely heroine, she is an arresting character who rises to tragic stature as she fights her way to personal peace. It is doubtful, however, that Duley created her as a mythic Newfoundland figure; Josephine Keilly seems to fit that role better. Although Mageila's country is in her, she is beyond place; and, as such, she is Duley's ideal woman.

In spite of his being used as a butt for Duley's dislike of Commission of Government, Trevor Morgan is the most likeable of her heroes. Although she found deep satisfaction in the ties with the British Monarchy, Duley was mortified to think that a proud people like Newfoundlanders were considered unfit to rule themselves. As a result, Trevor is recognized immediately by his accent as "one of them English fellas runnin' us now." Likewise, his admission that he is "a lesser bit of the system" elicits an edged reply from a testy patriot:

> 'And a mighty poor system it is . . . You fellahs don't know a fish-tail from a turnip. Agriculture, me eye! This country must live or die by its fishery. Yes, sir . . . Richer than the mines of Peru! That's what they said about the cod-fishery and they took damn good care they lined their own pockets with it. If you gave us a million a minute now, it wouldn't make up for what you did to us in . . . What we want is somebody who understands the *fishery*! Ruined, that's what we are; and soon the grass
> —[22]

When Trevor says that the British are here now to make amends, Mageila's doubt is overt: "They say the Englishman governs like the cock who thinks the sun rises to hear him crow." One is not surprised to learn that Duley once told a friend that she was going to write a book called *Mad Dogs and Englishmen*. Yet on the whole Trevor Morgan fares better than the other heroes in her novels; for example, at the end he emerges from his predicament more gracefully than Murray Blair does in *Novelty on Earth*. Trevor shows the kind of spirit that Duley seems to admire. When he hears from his wife that she will not divorce him, he says to Mageila, "England or no England I won't go back to her". He will return home to fight in the war; and when it is all over he may be able to return. In this way, Duley lets him keep his self-respect; but she is not always so charitable.

The other characters in *Highway to Valour* are particularly effective because the author has a considerable talent for differentiating among temperaments; and she achieves her best effects by sharp contrasts on a diminishing though never trivial scale. Unlike her royal ancestress, for example, Sheila Mageila is a religious tartar whose every Sunday is a "Praise — God — Barebones day" of spiritual battle. The fire of her life is stoked by testimonies, prayer meetings, child-raising, house-scouring and bossing. As such a stiff Sankey-Moodie woman, she can soften only to her joyous French husband. Mageila thinks that her mother does not love her daughters: "We were only faces to wash and stockings to darn. But I know she loved Papa." With unshakable persistence, Mrs. Michelet does her duty in all things, such as quelling Pea-Pea Peter's rum binges by a tart remonstrance, rationing the French folk-songs at home and choosing carefully her girls' selections for the school concerts. Mageila's life seems to be directed by the bas-relief of one of the Wesley brothers whose protruding lip she considers to be "the very thrust of Methodism," as well as by her mother's sharp directives to sing "I should like to die said Willie" and "Jesus wants me for a sunbeam." In spite of her constrictive beliefs concerning the leading of saved sinners in prayer and her unchallenged position on the organ stool of the Methodist Church where she pedals with her feet and strikes with her hands to bring "forth a loud noise unto the Lord," Sheila Mageila wears pretty night-gowns sprigged with flowers and likes her husband's compliments. When she faces death her courage is immense, as Mrs. Slater indicates: "I saw her standing like a rock, with her daughters hanging round her neck."

Mrs. Michelet's husband is a slipshod Roman Catholic from St. Pierre, the French island off the South Coast of Newfoundland, where there are "Frenchmen, and not French-Canadians." Since the Dilkes lived around Fortune Bay, a few hours' boat ride from St. Pierre, it would not be unusual for the two nationalities to meet. As a result, in Duley's novel, the easy-going Frenchman "capitulated at once to [Sheila Mageila's] snug charms" by marrying into the Wesleyans without a frown from the neighbours because he went inside a Catholic church only when he "went to town to buy his supplies, and to his own French island." There were obviously no Roman Catholics in Feather-the-Nest to trouble his conscience. A good deal of Newfoundland's geography is a patchwork quilt of religions. Name the area and one knows the denomination. To Mageila Pierre is "a man from a minted sovereign." Sharply distinct from his authoritarian wife, he has a "mind profile under skin as clear as golden-oak," as well as a great capacity for gaiety, love, serenity and *crème de menthe* toddies. His little celebrations, his teasing, his sensitivity in forbidding his wife to put dogberries in her crab-apple jelly ("No, Mama, no! You must not boil the berries belonging to the birds"), his un-Wesleyan laughter and his resistance to being detained for second meeting ("with a liberated step [he] went home to do what he liked and to listen to the Catholic hour") make him a lovable character. Duley thus provides an unforgettable picture of a father romping with his daughters as he sings for them "Sur le Pont d'Avignon":

> . . . in his most abandoned moods he would sing 'Les belles dames font comme ça' and the little girls would curtsey, and again when he sang 'Les braves soldats font comme ça' they would salute and then organ-grind . . .[23]

By contrast, Duley treats the religiosity of Methodism with malicious humour and often with outright derision. Sister Waddleton, for example, is shown in all her pretentiousness:

> She was impressive, suggestive of murky opulence, ostrich-features, and five-gore skirts; and she was a twice-saved sinner: once in South America, where the boulevards of Brazil had not kept her steadfast; then in Feather-the-Nest where the rocks brought her back to the Lord and the seas cleansed her thoughts of Rio. Her voice was unctuous, soft, and her accent grand when she spoke intimately of 'Gawd' and the 'awcid test.'[24]

After the tidal wave, Mrs. Waddleton's voice, which sounds "like thick white grease," worries the bereaved people with its vulgarity, especially as it reminds them of her tactless self-election as their chief comforter and prayer leader. While one laughs or even shudders at Mrs. Waddleton's exhibitionism, however, one admires Mrs. Slater because she is a crook-backed, withered, old woman who speaks the language of the Bible lovingly and with Godlike serenity so that she is likened to "a chapter in Isaiah." Mageila asks her if she is lonely living by herself far up on the hill; and she replies: "I am not alone, my maid." It is this simple, tranquil and wise woman who steeps strong tea for the survivors of the tidal wave, cleans out the cuts of frightened children and carries a sheep with a broken leg up the crunching path to her door; and it is she who forces Mageila to face reality and to take her first step along her highway to valour: "I'd take your trouble if I could but I'm at the other end of sorrow. Useless to tell you now that morning will come again." As she wrote to Ellen Elliott in December 1940, Duley was pleased that the readers at Macmillan had "praised the magnificent old woman, Mrs. Slater [for] — she is my own memory of my grandmother." Saintly Mrs. Slater is one of the most important characters in the book because she is a symbol of hope and perseverance. Thus Mageila compares her to a rock; indeed, she even "looked like me, dark with iron-stains" as she pointed Mageila in the right direction on the road to valour:

"Next to richness of loved ones on earth is the richness of loved ones in Heaven. I find it hard to separate the two worlds, but you're young for that. In time it will become softer." In addition to one of Duley's grandmothers, there may also be in the character of Mrs. Slater an indirect tribute to Nurse D. Cherry of the Nonia Centre at Lamaline.[25] Since contemporary newspapers were full of stories concerning her courage and goodness, she became known as "the Florence Nightingale of the disaster".

The rank and file of the Feather-the-Nest characters are briefly but vividly sketched: there is Sister Clark at the prayer meetings with her blackened teeth and bad breath; there is Uncle Mosey Rowden, refusing to testify standing up and elaborately spreading a red handkerchief for his knees before uttering a loud "Hallelujah"; there is Pea-Pea Peter, sitting at the back of the church because he has to go out so often; and finally there are the overwrought women who cry out in many tongues as Mageila's sisters stuff handkerchiefs into their mouths to keep from laughing.

With the exception of Captain Dilke, the Ship-Haven characters are slight figures who are interesting only as embodiments of the upper crust of out-harbour society. Molly, who thinks it a disgrace to be sick or to take a laxative, regards boiled fowl and white sauce as a panacea for grief; and, as such, she reminds one of Samuel Butler's Erewhonians who put sick people in jail because they have no business being unfortunate in their constitutions. Ella, who likes to talk about her major operation, is the most peace-loving sister. Beatie, whose hat is too smart for a minister's wife in mourning, does not make her husband wash enough and has no time for faints. All three sisters are self-important because they belong to an old outport family and have in them a rich vein of what Thackeray might call "Snob-ore." As a result, they are fanatical housekeepers and political ostriches, who are so unshakably naive that they think Hitler is "a very bad man who might have been saved through church-work"; and, in any case, they seem to think that there simply cannot be a second World War. Similarly, they cannot understand how a young girl such as Mageila can sit still for so long listening to opera or reading books. With a dash of that ghoulish humour with which she often seasons her satire, Duley writes that, "All the Dilkes had read *The Mill on the Floss*, and [that] they knew Mageila would appreciate it as everyone in it was drowned." Although one glimpses the husbands only fleetingly, the Reverend Leander White, "a tall gangling man with the rutted face of a Lincoln," is very memorable.

Of this group only the octogenarian grandfather has important dramatic stature. Mageila says that "he would invite the King of England to eat salt fish with him and expect him to like it . . . He doesn't believe in the fatted-calf welcome." The old man does not quail before adverse fortune. If Poseidon is ruler of the ocean, Captain Dilke pays him no homage, but his clear blue eyes are always ready to meet those of the hostile god of the seaquakes.

The serio-comic encounter with the terrible flies that draw blood from tortured necks and especially from Dr. Britten's is an example of ways in which

Duley makes use of her friends to help her create memorable types. For the elderly Dr. Britten, the indefatigable botanist, is probably an affectionate recollection of Stanley Truman Brooks, the young Curator of Recent Invertebrates, and later Director, at the Carnegie Museum in Pittsburgh, Pennsylvania, who made three expeditions to Newfoundland and Labrador during the period 1935 to 1939 with his wife Betty Watts Brooks, an entomologist.[26] During these visits, they were well-known and liked in St. John's, where mild jokes circulated about their collecting bugs, snails, and molluscs.

When Mageila moves to St. John's, the reader is given an unflattering picture of the élite by one of its own members. Unlike the Fitz Henrys in *Cold Pastoral*, Mrs. Kirke is very critical of her peers. Tied to a war-shattered husband, who is killing himself with alcohol and drugs, she hires Mageila to teach French to her little girl. The two women have long conversations in the course of which the older woman becomes Duley's mouth-piece against social pretension and the futility of war:

> My friends are absurd. Like most Newfoundlanders, their forebears came from England and *all* their possessions tied up in a red pocket handkerchief; but now their descendants have a tremendous sense of property. My sister is very helpful in establishing a privileged class.[27]

Such people, like Trevor Morgan's wife in England, Mrs. Kirke claims, "would die if she had to eat macaroni and cheese for supper, *in Newfoundland* at six-thirty." Duley digs more than a spade-depth to expose the niggling minds of the élite of colonial St. John's; they are people who will not permit library books to come into their homes because of the germs on them or whose children are not allowed to play jackstones because it will give them knuckles. "Stiffy-staffy" and "The Dog Takes a Bone" are obviously games for the lower orders, and not for those who go to English schools. As a consequence, the Kirke boys are taken from their school and sent to Canada because their mother believes that in Neville Chamberlain's England students are being educated in unreality, and thus blinded to the imminence of a second world war.

St. John's, with its air thick with the incense of colonialism, seems as reprehensible as Britain to Mrs. Kirke:

> Everybody knows everyone in St. John's — at least, my sister would add, who's anyone and, of course, who's anyone English, and your Trevor is included because he's got the rich voice. England is convenient. You don't need a social register — just the book that reports their salaries in case they're marriageable. We all went to English schools . . . Many of us know England is a fen of stagnant waters, but we want to be born in the fen.[28]

Duley's ambivalence towards England is as manifest in such passages as is her love-hate relationship with Newfoundland, as well as her mockery of the very houses she frequented. Although she played the social game and ran with the right set, deep down she mistrusted their fripperies.

As a result, Mrs. Kirke's relatives are limned in the novel just as the Dilke sisters are. The best at behaving in a grand fashion is Mrs. Langley, a stout, marcelled Colonial who would like to be English and who has taken to wearing pastel shades since the royal visit of George VI and Queen Elizabeth in 1939; and as a result she "would never be satisfied until she had a fanlight over her door, etc., etc." A lavish entertainer, she is perplexed when Mageila takes Patricia to a children's party at her house. Should the girl sit with the mothers or be sent to the kitchen with the maids? Mageila quietly upstages the hostess by going for a walk. Tart as a crab-apple, the author continues to disparage her class, particularly those middle-aged women "whose heads were curled and whose feet winced from the ground in high-heeled pain", as well as those who "had so much leisure that they liked running a funeral," and those who "were even enjoying the war because it gave them something to do."

Mrs. Kirke's character embodies Duley's most sustained attack on war. Mr. Kirke is a piece of human flotsam from the 1918 carnage whose yellow, skull-like face is a reminder of what war does to people. As there seems to be nobody to stop Hitler, Mrs. Kirke is eloquent in her frustration:

> England is asleep! As Priestley says, she's become a nation of inheritors. But the Solomon Slows are going to have a terrible awakening and while they are feeling profoundly shattered the beautiful boys will go out and die because the deluded old men had no foresight. How pleasant war would be if the right people could be shot.[29]

The malignity and absurdity of the world confound Mr. Kirke: "Hills stuck up, a great deal of untidy water, odd animals on all fours, ordinary humans on two legs and subhuman ones goose-stepping like terrible dolls . . . Our sins are many, but we can still speak out loud. Imagine not being able to express your loathing of Nazi necks because your own might end on the block." Mageila too sees the paradoxes as she tells Trevor that she does not want to volunteer as a VAD when the war comes because "Shooting people and trying to mend them is most unnatural for a natural faculty."

As acrid as is the anti-war note in the novel, the author, however, is never contemptuous of heroes. When Mageila mourns her father's death in his attempt to reach her doomed mother and sisters, her grandfather reminds her that one's life can become a gift to others: "I remember a fellow in the war who lost his legs, and when someone like Leander sympathized with him he said he didn't lose his legs — he gave them." And Mr. Kirke, who is perhaps partially modelled on Nelson Duley, is never repulsive to Brin, his faithful dog, nor to Mrs. Kirke, who softens to tears and blames herself for letting the housekeeper "hide him away so much," and for having been "such a coward about his smells, and the way he had to scratch his hands." In view of her regrets, one is not convinced by Mrs. Kirke's bitterness that she cannot leave her husband because there is no divorce in Newfoundland. Legal separations were available; and if she could afford to send her boys to Canadian boarding schools, she could afford to put her case to the Canadian courts. She remains with her husband probably because, as Moira Brophy says, "There's nothing but the lunatic-asylum and that's no place for the poor man." Thus it is loyalty, and not the absence of divorce laws, which keeps Mrs. Kirke at home. Similarly, even though there is divorce in England, Trevor's wife will not release him to marry Mageila.

Moira Brophy, the Kirke's maid, is Duley's best servant character. She is "the most unmoral person living and as sweet as natural sap"; she rules her mistress and deals with every situation; and she accepts drugs, drunkenness, Hitler, Stalin, and Mussolini as the will of God. Her philosophy is simple: when the alcoholic is past redemption, give him all he wants and more; when the drug addict is incurable, pass him the needle for "God would take care of their foolishness." Her grey hair is the only thing that she does not regard as the will of God. As a result, she dyes it black to match the lock which her "fellah" took to war in his prayer-book, and which she told him to button up in his breast-pocket, so that no bullet could get by: "But there's other parts of a man to hit, Miss; so he was killed . . . I'm not taking chances on him not knowing me when I walk into Heaven. He left me black, and black I'll stay." Moira drowns kittens in a toilet bowl, and "grotesque in a barrel-shaped night-dress bends to let the dog Brin into the smoke of his master's bedroom to die with him, making no attempt to rescue, because it must be a God-given opportunity that the dinner platter beside the bed did not catch all Mr. Kirke's cigarette ash." She forces Mageila and Mrs. Kirke back from the door, and never once scruples that she may have deliberately killed a man: 'Like sea-water, opaque over its own secrets, Moira's eyes cleared for a moment, revealing frightening depths."

The multiple setting does not disturb the structure of the book as it does in *Cold Pastoral* because *Highway to Valour* has a coherence and vision that the earlier story lacks. The theme of valour and Mageila's fight for self-control and spiritual peace move along a highway that stretches from Feather-the-Nest and Ship-Haven to Labrador and St. John's; and the sea is near all of these places. The Kirke household does not cause any break in the progression because their suffering is linked to Mageila's through the two world wars that impinge on each other; the first in the tragic figure of Mr. Kirke, and the second in the Kirke boys who, as well as Trevor Morgan, will have to fight.

The emphasis on the capital city as a high town "with four hill-drops to the sea", the glimpse of the train rushing along a river and over a trestle as it bears Captain Dilke home, the climbing tram-cars, church spires, the long line of the harbour filled with tall masts, the steep, winding road to Signal Hill, Cabot Tower and the open Atlantic, and the lighthouse at Cape Spear are images that become extensions of the height and effort which began with the hill of water of the tidal wave. These images of the town that are drawn from a natural setting evoke ties with the outports and are thus a powerful force in developing the story of Mageila's journey over a series of ascents to the final one on the headlands of Labrador. As a result, she can accept the partiality of both the land and the sea; indeed, the latter will always be the same "with other people travelling over it; and all of them will want something permanent and more of them will find it." But the saving grace is the fact that the "ones who love will know that they can walk through the waters and not feel drowned."

Water is used in the book as an expanding symbol of the two sides of nature. The sea is the mystery that is life as the gift-bearer and the despoiler; and, in addition, it reflects the inscrutability of God as the element that both drowns and baptizes into new life. As such, it is Mageila's agony as well as her salvation. Hence the reader can see it through her eyes as "she wept for the rage of water." For Mageila, it was pitiless and hostile as it crossed the road to lick at doors; and as it "lifted like a scythe to reap the land" and a "foaming cauldron . . . holding the sprawling limbs and streaming hair" of the dead; likewise, it became "a big blurred being with slobbering lips"; and finally, an "engulfing darkness" in which Mageila was immersed as she tried to cure the pain of the tidal wave's victims whose "death struggles shattered her." Although water quenches "the beautiful lights where I would always be looking,"[30] it will not always darken life. Because Mrs. Slater represents hope, she rallies Mageila with her cry, "Rise up, my maid," and with her quotation from Isaiah, "When thou passest through the waters I will be with thee: and through the rivers they shall not overflow thee . . . When thou walkest through the fire thou shalt not be burned."

The malice of oceans is mitigated in the novel by their kinder moods. Sea and sky therefore show shades that range from oyster green, soft grey, pearly white to deep blue. The *Assou* glides one morning among hundreds of icebergs; and "so quiet was its course that it looked like a hearse winding between mighty tomb-stones" so that it seemed to be "like memorials for men like Columbus, Cabot, Cartier." Death and life are made companionable in these and other images:

> Beauty was intense, fierce, with a colour announcing that ice was never white. The mighty bergs rose high, with steep aquamarine sides running with rainbow water from the heat of the sun . . .
> 'They're upside down in the sky,' breathed Mageila.
> It was true. The ice-bergs were inverted in the blue sky above the horizon, making a picture like an ecstatic day in an ice-age.[31]

This aquamarine day is followed by a night of Northern Lights. The Eskimos believe that they are "long lights to guide the dead across the dark valley"; and the sailors and the passengers are entranced by the rainbow hues so different from the greenish yellow ones of St. John's. A former skipper of the *Kyle* told me that his crew always said that if you whistled at the lights they danced. In Duley's book, Trevor Morgan uses such knowledge when he calls the Northern Lights "The Dancers."

The sea that destroys her family paradoxically brings Mageila the comfort of memories of her sisters and her father on the beach; thus she recalls him "scrunching stones with his big feet"; while the sun would be "a fire-ball burning the sea, and they would run in the glare, follow the waves out over wet stones, retreat when they turned and chased their feet. They would laugh and leap from rock to rock, get splashed and not feel the splashing."[32] In this way, the moods of the ocean are woven closely into the fabric of Duley's book. Crimson washes through the novel in the images of injuries after the disaster such as the fly-bitten flesh in Labrador and the blood-red sun. Like a fiercely representational painting, the scene at the whaling station is as disgusting as a festering wound when eight bloated, dead whales are moored to a raft ready for disembowelment by the cutter. The whales' huge, swollen bodies which expel air, water and blood as the huge knives slice into them are a fitting symbol of the grotesqueries of natural disasters, slaughter houses and of war. The sight of these majestic mammals thus humiliated in a public spectacle is a prevision of the blood to be spilled in the coming war: "Surely no dictator could make masses of boys mix their blood with earth and the salt of the sea." Similarly, the slaughter of the whales is linked with "the savage battles of the forests" as imaged in the interlocked stags' horns in the Dilke house. Duley's awareness of the cruelty of nature is thus expressed in terms of blood and water. There is also a touch in the book of what one might call Crucifixion imagery: Mageila's eyes, for example, are "nailed" as she fixes them on her doomed house and feels "that they must crucify on Feather-Cake with its points leaning for a last look at the land"; and in addition, she weeps for Christ as she reads Renan's *Vie de Jésus*. Blood, water, and upheaval of the elements as images of Calvary are also integral to the events in Mageila's life. In this way, one may view *Highway to Valour* as a Way of the Cross on a human level with a resurrection for the heroine at the end.

With the exception of a few florid passages, the style of the book is controlled and lyrical. The Newfoundland dialect is reproduced without condescension or strain as is evident in the following examples: "And how it riz! B'y, how it riz . . .! I seen the boats lift up, the fish-flakes go, and two cows"; "Shut yer trap . . . 'Tis easy for the likes of you, insured like y're for an Act of God"; "I was in the last war m'self. Had m' members frost-bit in Gallipoli"; "Some gets bit so bad they get p'isoned. Some don't get bit at all. You'd think, sir, their flesh was a bit high. I had a woman last year — took on something awful, and at last she wound herself up in toilet-paper like one of them corpses they fancy-up, and then she complained the flies bit through the j'ins."

French is used not only for melodic effects but also to contrast characters and points of view. Early in the novel Pierre Michelet's songs and conversations with his daughters represent the joy that is absent from Sheila Mageila's Methodism:

> When Mageila was very young, asking how she could be the seventh daughter when there were only five, her mother explained that two had gone to glory. But her French father said, with a tiny smile, "Elles sont au ciel, ma chérie".[33]

Similarly, Biblical echoes heighten the theme of valour. Duley not only quotes directly, but she also absorbs the cadences of Scripture into the speech of some of her characters. Mrs. Slater, for example, sounds like a psalm:

> Times come when God seems far away. I'd take your trouble if I

could, because I am at the other end of sorrow. Useless to tell you now that morning will come again . . . . Where can you go, my maid, out of sight of the sea? When people came to this country they did not come for the land. The sea gives and the sea takes away, and for the fat years it demands its lean years . . .[34]

All the large happenings and important moments of the book call forth the resonances of the Bible. Mageila's agony, for instance, as she gazes after her drowning home is expressed like a sacred song: "God, God, let me cure pain now if ever I cured it before. Their flesh is my flesh. Let their pain come into me so that my hands can touch it and I can mix myself with their death." Similarly, her premonition of meeting Trevor alludes to the *Song of Solomon:* "He took me to a banqueting house and his banner over me was love"; and when they part, she expresses her feelings in Biblical terms: "The ones who love will know they can walk through the waters and not feel drowned."

Highway to Valour is powerful because it looks tragedy squarely in the face. Duley's sense of life's double-dealing allows her to offer Mageila a tempered happiness at the end of the book, so that in a sense both she and her heroine have come to terms with the harshness of Newfoundland. Trevor Morgan's declarations that "Your country is in you, Mageila" and that "people in the town . . . They never represent a country" are therefore more convincing than Mater's tentative remark to Philip that Mary Immaculate "perhaps bears out your father's theory that the best blood in this country is in the Bays." *Highway to Valour* is Duley's repudiation of the theme of escape in her two earlier novels, as well as her espousal of her homeland for better or for worse. Isabel Pyke has to die to solve her problems; Mary Immaculate fools herself that she is still attached to "the Cove"; and Mageila is at peace because she does not divide Newfoundland into sections, and because she will work where she is most needed whether by great waters or in the narrower confines of the city. The book has a vision that the other two lack because, like *Novelty on Earth*, it transcends parochial sorrows and the plight of lovers parted.

1. All letters to or from Ellen Elliott and Marguerite Lovat Dickson that are quoted in this book are from the Macmillan File.
2. Two native Newfoundlanders, Anastasia English (1864-1959) and Erle Spencer (1897-1937), had some success with fiction. The one wrote innocuous romances; the other, whom Margaret Duley knew through "hearsay memory", focused on sea stories. They were not known on the Canadian mainland.
3. (4 October 1941), p. 8.
4. (28 September 1941), p. 26.
5. (11 October 1941), p. 13.
6. (27 September 1941), p. 10.
7. (27 September 1941), p. 24.
8. Documentation in Duley's scrapbook is incomplete.
9. English-Canadian Letters, 1941: ed. A.S.P. Woodhouse, II Fiction by J. R. MacGillivray, *University of Toronto Quarterly* (April 1942), p. 304.
10. In the final version called simply Mageila and her mother Sheila Mageila.

Thomas and Tryphena Duley
or
Margaret's father and mother

The Duley Children

Margaret (Great Aunt Chancey) and Lionel Thomas Chancey

Margaret and Gladys

51.

*Rennies Mill
Road*

Gladys, Mrs. Duley and Margaret

Captain Cyril Duley

Nelson Duley

Margaret: 1941

Margaret left; Harford Powel at microphone

Freda Jefferies and Margaret, Aunt Alice in car. Somerset 1953

Freda

Florence Duley and daughter Margot

Margot Duley and her husband Lance Morrow

Gladys and her daughter Margaret Crowell

Marshall Courtney

11. See *The Evening Telegram* from 23 November to 30 November 1929.
12. For some published sources on Sheila NaGeira see Herbert Halpert 'Ireland, Sheila and Newfoundland' in *Literature and Folk Culture: Ireland and Newfoundland* ed. Alison Feder and Bernice Schrank, Memorial University Folklore and Language Publication Series Bibliographical and Special series, No. 2, 1977, pp 147-48. Also same in Memorial University of Newfoundland Reprint Series, No. 3, 1979.
13. *Highway to Valour*, pp. 26-27.
14. *Ibid.*, p. 47.
15. Now a rusting derelic in Harbour Grace.
16. Trevor watches the mail-boat being lowered. See p. 164.
17. Captain Edward O'Keefe, former skipper of the *Kyle*, told me this.
18. *Highway to Valour*, p. 196.
19. *Ibid.*, p. 102-03.
20. *Ibid.*, p. 5.
21. *Ibid.*, p. 285.
22. *Ibid.*, p. 112.
23. *Ibid.*, p. 10.
24. *Ibid.*, p. 15.
25. Nonia stands for Newfoundland Outport Nursing and Industrial Association. It was organized in 1924 to provide fully-trained nurses and midwives for the remote areas of Newfoundland, and to encourage home industries; and it still produces fine woven and knitted goods so that the Nonia shop on Water Street is a tourist attraction.
26. Stanley Truman Brooks, 'Across Newfoundland,' *Natural History* (December 1935), pp. 417-30; see also Pittsburgh *Post Gazette* (1 April 1939), p. 99. Brooks also wrote poetry. See his *Above the Smoke* (Philadelphia, Dorrance and Company 1937).
27. *Highway to Valour*, p. 238.
28. *Ibid.*, p. 240.
29. Ibid., p. 213.
30. See epigraph, p. 40.
31. *Highway to Valour*, p. 156.
32. *Ibid.*, p. 224.
33. *Ibid.*, p. 5.
34. *Ibid.*, pp. 58; 63.

CHAPTER SIX

Novelty on Earth

Although *Novelty on Earth* (first called *Older than Eden*) was not published until 1942, it was written before *Highway to Valour* as Duley indicated to Ellen Elliott in a letter of December 1940 about a month after she had submitted *Highway to Valour* to Macmillan:

> I have a sleek beautiful novel called "Novelty on Earth" which is in quite a different genre from "Highway to Valour". It is sophisticated, with a sting in its tail but never acid — How do Macmillans react to the full blaze of the woman's angle in life — written with warm-hearted candour — & with emotion but no sentimentality — ?

It is clear that the finished manuscript of *Novelty on Earth* was sent to Hutchinson in England before Macmillan especially since Ellen Elliott wrote to Duley in March, 1941 to find out if her contract with Hutchinson was null and void; if it was still in effect Macmillan could not publish either *Highway to Valour* or *Novelty on Earth* because publisher's protocol demanded that the English firm be given first choice. On 17 March Duley replied that she was "quite free of that company"; and she further disclosed that she had sent *Novelty on Earth* to Hutchinson before offering it to Macmillan. The tone of Duley's letter suggests a deterioration in her relationship with the English firm: Hutchinsons, she reports, "had Novelty on Earth & sent it back — saying it had too much conversation — Then I recalled it from England myself — in view of the circumstances."

Macmillan reacted variously to the manuscript. Marguerite Lovat Dickson put her seal of approval on it for its wit, its depth of feeling, and its interesting study of woman. Ann Foster of the Publicity Department said that it was the very finest Canadian manuscript she had ever read and that its psychological analysis reminded her of Claude Houghton's *Neighbours*. Ellen Elliot was enchanted with it; Mr. Wheeler, the second official reader, seemed to like it although his remarks are not on record. Only F.A. Upjohn seemed to balk at it, for he thought that the hero, John Murray Blair, was unconvincing, that the author allowed her artistic sense to be influenced by some sort of personal feeling, and that there was too much infelicitous phraseology. Blair took strong exception to "They became receiving sets and amplifiers for intangible things" as a description of the quick rapport between the lovers; and he also disliked the following: "Her voice trailed away like the long retreat of a bolster"; "Children fidgeted with hands belonging to land distraction"; "His chair had become a spring-board expelling him to the window"; and "Pure and fine with the lips of a boy, life dripped from his eyes." Duley's blotting-paper imagery made Blair particularly unhappy: "His eyes looked like blotting paper for her rich vitality"; "She was too tough to let her body become a blotting-paper of concern for suffering she would willingly endure herself"; and finally "blotting-paper for their pity."

Blair's concern about the style was responsible for a memorable reference to and comment by E. J. Pratt. Mr. Upjohn, who had been trying out some of these Duleyisms on his friends, wrote to Ellen Elliott for her professional opinion. While he was dictating this letter on 23 March 1941, Pratt came into his office:

> I have read him some of the similes, although it was perhaps hardly fair to do so when he knows nothing about the book or the context from which they have been taken. He does feel, however, that all the blotting paper should be thrown out the window or perhaps even a handier place where it is less likely to be easily retrieved.

Actually Duley dined with the Pratts when she was in Toronto early in 1941. About forty years later, Pratt's widow, Viola, recalled the novelist as a dark, rather intense person who did not talk as much as some of the other guests but "whom we found interesting." In fact, Mrs. Pratt found her more pleasant than most of the authors that her hospitable husband brought home for meals and conversation; and it is also pleasant to realize that Pratt and Duley shared a great fondness for dogs.

Meanwhile, Upjohn's objections had little effect on the published book, for it contains nearly all of the phrases that he had condemned. The author had obviously not given way to these criticisms any more than she had to those about the cats in *Highway to Valour*. Such recalcitrance seems to have been part of her nature. After publishing *Highway to Valour* and *Novelty on Earth*, Macmillan dropped their option on her next novel, *Octaves of Dawn*, probably because she was not prepared to change her tack. When it came to accepting criticism of her work, she was often stubborn; so there is probably some truth in the remark by a friend that Duley was uncritical of her own work.

Published in New York in the spring of 1942, *Novelty on Earth* was also issued in Canada with the imprint of the Macmillan Company of Toronto. The novel had a wide circulation and was reviewed favourably in many newspapers and periodicals including the *New York Times Book Review*.[1] Toronto's *Saturday Night* made the most perceptive remarks about the book:

> It is a novel for adult minds only; her perception is too subtle and her understanding of human problems has clearly been the fruit of too considerable a life experience for it to be redigested by sluggish readers

in search of soluble pills of knowledge. But there is gaiety too; minor flights of fancy and shafts of wit illuminate the whole. A book to buy and treasure and re-read.[2]

Novelty on Earth probably had better sales than Duley's other novels. In 1944 Methuen and Company published it in England under the title *Green Afternoon* and sold two thousand copies within a year; and in 1946 it was published in a Swedish translation as *Sö Stred Sara (How Sara Struggled)*. By 1956 Macmillan had only twelve copies unsold so there is no doubt that by this time the author was at the peak of her career.

It is interesting to speculate on the fact that Duley changed from Milton to Swinburne for both the title and epigraph of the English edition. Perhaps "In the Orchard" suited her mood at a time when she wanted to stress the ecstasy rather than the mockery in the book:

The grass is thick and cool, it lets us lie.
Kissed upon either cheek and either eye,
    I turn to thee as some green afternoon
Turns towards sunset, and is loth to die;
Ah God, Ah God, that day should be so soon.

Or perhaps the publishers liked the sentence from the book, "It was green afternoon with the glare of noon sweetly sequestered"[3] and thought the description a neater fit for the war-standard size of their publications.

Novelty on Earth is very different from Duley's preceding novels. The hurtling seas, the rocky coastline of Newfoundland and the well-drawn outport characters give place to the locale of "any British colony" in summer when the laburnums glitter like topazes, and to autumn in London when the leaves change colour and fall. The lovers "lived this episode before Aryan blood was quite so important,[4] before the Germans wanted to go home, and all over the place at the same time . . . when there was comparative peace, and . . . when the diehards said that common sense would prevail." It is an absorbing story riding high on conversation, peopled with urbane men and women, and imbued with a delicate irony; all of which prevent the theme of adultery from being banal.

The title is taken from Book Ten of *Paradise Lost* where a peevish Adam, after the apple has been eaten, berates Eve and questions God's wisdom in creating woman:

Thus Adam to himself lamented loud . . .
Whom thus afflicted when sad Eve beheld
Desolate where she sat, approaching nigh
Soft words to his fierce passion she assayed;
But her with stern regard he thus repelled: —
    'Out of my sight thou serpent!
                    . . . Oh, why did God,
Creator wise, that peopled highest Heaven
With Spirits masculine, create at last
This novelty on Earth, this fair defect
Of Nature, and not fill the World at once

> With men as Angels, without feminine;
> Or find some other way to generate
> Mankind?'
>
> [11. 845-95]

It is obvious in the novel that Duley finds Milton's Adam to be very funny; and she uses him particularly as a whipping-boy in the figure of John Murray Blair. If Milton is a male chauvinist, Duley is a derisive feminist who manages to make Adam, Milton and Blair look foolish all at once. Milton is crucial to the ironic thrust of this novel in which paradise is lost because the man lacks the courage and honesty that Duley admires in her fictional Eve. In addition, her transposition of the Adam and Eve motif to a modern love affair is bold and effective.

The story is about an adulterous relationship which ends paradoxically with the wife who is unaware of the affair, in control, and with the mistress being victorious in defeat. Sara Colville is thirty-one, beautiful, brainy, twice-widowed, and a successful writer. She meets John Murray Blair at a ball at Government House, where they are instantly attracted to each other, and kiss through a handkerchief to avoid the tell-tale smear of lipstick that could reveal Murray's actions to his wife. This rather ludicrous occurrence is significant because it indicates how important it is for the man to protect his public reputation for the sake of his small son in England whom he idolizes. If, as she claims, Duley was once given such a kiss, it helps one to understand why she cannot seem to refrain from sniping at men in her novels.

Murray meets Sara when she is more aware than usual of "the everpresent need of something to colour and fortify life, something that could stand like a rock in shifting sands." Happy as she has been with her former husbands, she has never been fully in love. Now that she has met her soul-mate, she plunges deliriously into a rapturous sexual attachment, in spite of Nora's warning that the last thing ever a nice man will sacrifice is his own roof, wife and childen.

Duley certainly convinces the reader that there is love at first sight, and that Sara, for the first time in her life, wants a child:

> . . . Sara felt her veins scald with desire for conception. Though the man
> would come first, it would be the means of fastening hooks of steel in his
> love, and holding him with the fetters he forged himself.[5]

Later with feminine inconsistency, she is blind to Murray's necessity to remain within the fetters that he had forged for himself when his son was born. His wife had fastened her own hooks of steel into his love as both Sara and Duley instinctively thought proper. As a result the extraordinary heroine of the novel, having first made herself an absolute widow by tossing the pictures of her two former husbands into her trunk, asks her lover, on their first night together, to give her a child. Murray's gentle refusal underscores Duley's theme of man's timidity and woman's fearlessness.

> She respected the decision, and the fact that she had lost in a big gamble.
> But she could have made the father angle right with the child. Nowa-
> days there were so many places a man could die and leave a posthumous
> child. And they said men were gamblers! They weren't. They were too

impregnated with caution and suspicion. It took women to sound the
clarion! He accepted the sensual joy, and would not concede a child
without a name. And his greatest wish! Was he being utterly selfish for
Noel? There was this separateness of men and women. The story of the
creation was wrong. Woman was not made from man's rib. She was
dropped haphazard, into the Garden of Eden from some separate
planet.[6]

The subtlety of Duley's novel is maintained throughout by such totally unem-
barrassed and candid writing.

After a rapturous three months, Murray returns to England to an ailing son
and to a wife he does not love, thereby leaving Sara to pick up the pieces of her
life in the wake of Nora's requiem to men's faint hearts:

> . . . did you ever meet a man — father, brother, husband, who wouldn't
> detour a hundred miles to avoid being straight-forward with a woman?
> They have some fixed idea it means a scene . . . As long as they can get
> away with a clean pair of heels they won't dwell on the unwritten letter,
> the telephone call they should have made, the flowers they should have
> sent, the meeting that would have made all clear — Murray is only a
> man, a little nicer than most.[7]

Although Nora and Sara have essentially the same view of men, Nora is willing
to accept them as they are while Sara rasps her mind and spirit against their
intransigence. The heart of her Sir Galahad is not pure because he cannot
either put her before his child, or give her one as a gift of his love. Although her
intense idealization of their relationship puts undue strain upon this gentle
knight, Sara, who is bound to him body and soul, will allow no compromise:
"For weal or woe I feel he belongs to me."

After an emotional collapse, she rallies for a while; yet even in misery she is
incorrigible. When Nora doles out sleeping pills to her one at a time for fear she
may take an overdose, Sara laughs at her:

> Don't be a fool, Nor! In spite of the world's worst, I'd be hard put to take
> that escape. Tonight I might lie down in despair, and wake up big with
> hope. Why — why — Murray's wife might *die*. She's as mortal as I am
> isn't she?[8]

Nora's shocked protest elicits another direct reply:

> I'm just vulgarly honest, Nor. My gutter side! I happen to know what I
> want, and I wouldn't dream of sitting delicately by to observe all the nice
> feelings that consume so much time. If I saw her death notice, by hook
> or by crook I'd take the house next door, and when he was returning
> from the cemetery[9]

Despite this show of mettle, Sara spends some time in a nursing home that
appears to be modelled on a small private hospital run years ago by Miss
Southcott on Monkstown Road in St. John's. This very well-written interlude is
a piquant exposition of the realities and indignities of being a patient.

When Sara recovers, she and Nora go to England to give Nora time to make
up her mind about having another baby, and to give Sara a chance to prove that
in spite of the proximity of Murray she can live and write where she wishes.

Duley's description of the ocean voyage contains a small piece of sharp social comedy, which is a terse, witty commentary on shipboard types. After the voyage, the episodes in London are full of smart Piccadilly hotels, thick carpets, cocktails and rustling housecoats. Since Nora's husband has informed Murray of the women's arrival, it is inevitable that he and Sara should meet again. Ironically, Murray's son, for whom he has left her, has a permanently damaged heart, which will eventually make him a semi-invalid. Still in love with her and realizing too late that there is "a love that could shake the earth under a man's feet," Murray is now willing to give Sara the children she wants and to take her as his mistress. He refuses, however, to divorce his wife while the boy is alive. But Sara cannot accept this proposal and tells him why:

> Then it was so very right! Now if I did it, it would be subduing myself to your wish, because I was aching for your unhappiness, and that would be death to the feelings I had before. Murray, at heart all women love respectability, goodness and protection, but there must be times in many of their lives when they ask what I asked, because of some deep exultation of utter mating . . . We seemed like perfect mutuality, some great urge that gave me the courage to snatch something for myself and go on alone and bring up a child without a male parent. All I can be now is the traditional female, the woman who is self-sacrificing, maternal, pitiful, giving way because of the needs of a man. That would kill me! I would be the complacent wife when the ecstasy of wishing is over. I know nothing of the cause. I can only follow my heart, and know when it feels flat. Only the wide range of that first love could excuse the birth of a child out of bounds . . .[10]

Before this the reader has been prepared for Sara's refusal by the story of the gloves that she had as a child:

> The first spring day I wore them I lost one glove. I nearly broke my heart but I hunted for days until the time came when I knew one glove was no good so I threw it away. The next day the other came back.[11]

This malevolent hint that Murray is a recovered derelict is typical of Duley's technique by which she not only cuts men down to size but also reduces the grandiosity of the language of love. As a consequence, Sara realizes during their meeting in London that in spite of their "perfect mutuality," the relationship between them can never be the same again; as she remarks, "It's the disarray of loving. Life fumbling through us." Logic tells her that as she had been his mistress in the summer, she could also be his mistress in the winter; but with Sara intuition comes first. Instinctively she knows she cannot take up where they left off. Her rejection of Murray is therefore right for her, in spite of the melodramatic tone of her remark at the end of the novel: "I know beyond doubt I'm Murray's widow." While Sara's motives may even include revenge, there is no doubt that she is true to herself as she faces life afresh to write a new novel *Dark Sunshine*.

The characterization in *Novelty on Earth* is thoroughly proficient, just as its ideas are advanced, its style rare and its structure firm. The heroine of the novel is an original character, who is much like the author herself. It is interesting to note, therefore, that Marguerite Lovat Dickson and Ellen Elliott both thought that Duley herself was a mixture of Mageila and Sara. The impetuous rush of Sara's conversation, with its wit, unselfconsciousness and fitting use of literary allusion is calculated to defeat all who thrive on the commonplace and deplore the quixotic. A single exchange with her can include a discourse on the nuptial flight of the queen bee as she is pursued by thousands of drones, as well as a comment on a spring morning when "the tops of the trees were like lace, and the sun came out in a bowl of daffodils", and the observation that the Walrus ate more oysters than the Carpenter. Her lack of self-pity is perhaps enviable: "It was no time to be full of water like poor Ophelia." Her wry appraisal of the hospital, the nurses, the steel instruments, and her thoughts on sleeping opposite "an old man rattling and wheezing towards the grave" are both funny and horribly realistic. In a word, Sara is a chameleon of moods who is tender, frank and satiric, and who is particularly aware of the strange comedy of life.

As a close friend Nora Hervey is a fine foil for Sara; as Sara realizes, "If you can find a woman in the room who looks as if you could say an Ave to her face and lay a golf ball at her feet that will be Nora." Wise and realistic, Nora is happy with her children and with her handsome but unimaginative husband. In her uncomplicated serenity she has hardly a thought for the grand passion and the search for what Sara calls the enigma of living. Because she understands men as far as they can be understood, Nora does not worry herself too much about their shortcomings; she does, however, make some acid comments on their responsibility for creating wars. In addition, Nora's daughters, Jennifer and Rosamund, who are described as "angels", are also disarmingly real; and as such they are a tribute to Duley's power of observation and to her understanding of babyhood.

Margot Hilton, who is unmarried and as emancipated as Sara, also embodies Duley's own ideas about a woman who becomes a man's mistress without remorse: "You can't take what a man hasn't got . . . For Brian it is absolutely necessary to be first with a woman, but after marriage he became a means to motherhood, and when three children had arrived she moved out of his room to be with the children." Margot will not allow Brian, who is her employer, to support her and, in addition, she will not use their relationship to gain special privileges for herself such as arriving late for work. She is probably fashioned after Duley's wordly wise friend who left St. John's to relieve her boredom and become the mistress of an important man in Montreal. Margot Hilton is likely the character Mary Quinn referred to when she told me that Duley used her friends as prototypes and was so blatant in this particular case that the friendship nearly foundered. At any rate, there is no doubt that in the novel Margot is a main spokesperson for Duley's feminist ideas and she is certainly memorable as are all the women in Duley's work.

The minor characters in *Novelty on Earth* are also handled deftly. Mrs.

MacCurdle, the extra "help" who comes when Sara has guests, disappears quickly from the story but not from the mind. "Worn and lacklustre," Mrs MacCurdle is a valuable engraving in a gallery of female portraits: "She looked like a blackcrow of a woman: someone who should not walk abroad in blossom-time, but wait until the trees were skeleton ghosts again." Pretty in her youth, she had married a man who drank. Her frank cynicism as she stirs the cheese sauce and attempts to disillusion Annie the maid, who is smitten with a sailor, is a sharp addition to a book that deliberately attacks man and gives him as good a look at himself as he is ever likely to get. Her husband gave her too many children: "MacCurdle was a Catholic and when he went to Confession he liked to think there was something he hadn't done . . . and nobody pays me for a fallen womb." But Annie is not to be deterred by Mrs. MacCurdle's warnings. As a young and healthy woman, she will have a fling with her sailor and probably go back to Alf, her fiancé, who drives a taxi. With an arresting turn of phrase, she does her bit to smudge the image of men. Alf's jealousy makes him fighting mad, perhaps because "he sits down all day, and he must be glad to stand up." Yet Annie cannot give him up:

> But I tried a total abstainer and that was worse. He thought smoking was a sin, and walking sprightly on Sundays. Then when he kissed me too hard he kept apologising, as if that was wrong too . . . he was more trouble to himself than he was to me . . . As for the lot of them, I could keep myself better any day, but a girl must get married sometime, and there's nothing to marry but what they call men.[12]

Although skivvies and tweenies were kept in their place in the Edwardian Duley household, the author allows them in her novels to have as piquant a point of view and as flavoursome a turn of phrase as their betters. Duley also uses them as grist to her mill for grinding men, for it is always the women who are the luminaries in her books.

For all his blond good looks, unshakable paternity and beautiful manners, John Murray Blair is an offending Adam. His head rules his heart, and that for Sara is the cardinal sin. While she believes that too much heart can make one do foolish things, she is convinced that too much head can make one ruthless because "it limits one's capacity to soar." Although Sara's expectations seem extravagent, she is prepared to risk a great deal more than Murray is. She thinks that if he had more children,[13] he would be a good father; whereas with one he is a fanatical father. At any rate, his love for his son is not altogether disinterested because young Noel becomes a substitute faith, or perhaps a glimpse of immortality for his atheistic father. As complex and as sincere as his stand seems to be, Murray's image is irreparably tarnished by the author's ruthless presentation of what she terms his betrayal. Thus he leaves Sara "with his beautiful mouth going into the twisted simile of a nice man who knows he is being a Judas for his special conception of thirty pieces of silver. She ached for his shame, and the expression of his face that a woman would rather not see." There is a streak of relentless egoism in a woman who equates a man's son with the blood money that sold Christ to the Cross. Yet Sara does not excuse herself for such untempered freedom of thought. The reader is led to believe that if Murray were Abraham and Noel, Isaac, Sara would not use the divine attribute of mercy to stay the father's hand. As an epigraph for Chapter Six, Duley uses the "spotless reputation" passage from Shakespeare for its ironic implication for her novel:

> The purest treasure mortal times afford
> Is spotless reputation; that away,
> Men are but gilded loam or painted clay.

In the novel, Murray's reputation is intact; perhaps shamefully so the reader feels because, having spent the night in Sara's bed, he hides behind her door in the morning and watches her rush to rescue young Jennifer Hervey who has tumbled into the lake. Although Sara may continue to love him, Duley makes it perfectly clear that the "Man's stock was down."

The questions the book raises are considerable, especially since they suggest that the author is a strong feminist and a free-thinker. In her writing, Duley casts a frosty eye on cant and tartly confronts the moral and social code by which she has been raised. In a word, these questions are just as important to the author as they are to the characters in her novel. Should a woman wear herself out bearing children? Should a wife overlook a husband's affair? Which is more important, the wife, or the child, in any set of circumstances? Why cannot a woman have a child out of wedlock and raise it without a father? Why have large families? Why not adopt and then "one can shop at the best places and complain about the nose and ears?" How can one balance the scales between too much head and too much heart? Should one limit one's capacity "to soar"? Is there perfect human love? When there is complex sexual mutuality, should lovers sacrifice themselves for others? Would wives be more loving if husbands were better lovers? Would husbands be faithful if wives were less maternal? Is Margot Hilton's worldly wisdom the proper treatment for "a mother-woman, who leaves her husband's bedroom for her children's."[14] Are ambition and virginity "two ice-cold qualities that foster the empty eye?" Why do parents try to possess children?" "Why do people make wars when nature wars strongest of all?" Why be fecund just to make an army?" As both Sara and Nora share the author's hatred of war and war mongers, they are as sharp as Lysistrata in defence of their own private Acropolis.

In the novel, the vigorous, unequivocal and sometimes intellectually naive answers to these questions seem to be prophetic of the New Morality or the Permissive Society of the present age; but they were viewed as particularly opprobrious in the Newfoundland of the thirties and forties. Early readers reacted strongly therefore to the expression of Duley's uninhibited ideas concerning theological and ethical subjects as when Sara and Murray argue vigorously about immortality.

The style of this book is an effective blend of conversation and humour. The humour is ironic, wry, mocking, extending to the grotesque and the macabre. The author loves to gall the kibes of men, and laughs barefacedly at the very types with whom she has always been well acquainted. She is very funny about English shoes that impart "a kind of pedestal base to a man." The British colonies are "backwaters where Englishmen go to consolidate" and to bind up "Empire sores in good English red-tape." Governors are made to appear ridiculous as their aides observe proper protocol in preparing them for a gala affair at Government House. The top English deputies, with their accents and their neckties from the best places, look like "exiles in the outer pale of Empire", while the lesser deputies are happy because they are meeting grander people than they would at home:

> It was beyond dispute that a ball at Government House was infinitely more glamorous than a whist-drive at Golders Green. With the wrong voices and ties, their more exalted countrymen thankfully threw them to the Colonials.[15]

Although the locale of the book may well be "any British colony, and the characters creations of the author's imagination" there is little doubt that Duley is laughing at the vice regal folderol that both attracted and bored her in St. John's. She wickedly reduces to a charade a Government House ball honouring the arrival in port of a Royal Navy cruiser: "Everybody who was anybody was there, and even some of the garden-party list was thrown in . . . Sofas and armchairs, tables and tabourets, seemed to have been wisked under Britannia's skirts, that her subjects might dance." The hearty Major-General, who makes it impossible for his partners to follow "his gay pas seul" and who thinks that the world would be better if more people were shot and if America could be exterminated because it gave the world cocktails and the League of Nations, is a parody of those dignified simpletons who "capitulated to poop-a-doop tunes" and tormented the ears and feet of polite women. It is noticeable that as Duley grew older she viewed the social round rather as a comedy of manners than as a serious pursuit. One friend distinctly remembers her at a garden party at Government House "looking elegant in flowing chiffon and a picture hat touring the grounds with gentlemen in grey toppers and making sedate conversation" and saying plaintively: "Don't you think we've wrung the last ounce out of it? Could we go now?" Her visits to Government House were very useful, however, for they provided her with dress rehearsals for similar scenes in her novels.

As well as satire, there is a good deal of drollery in *Novelty on Earth*. The descriptions of Sara's insomnia and her "trip" after an overdose of drugs are reckless and ruthless. Superb touches save the hospital scenes from bathos. Sleepless and full of wish-fulfillment, Sara identifies herself with the childbearing down the hall and, as a consequence, she longs for Murray. Irrelevantly, she remembers Cleopatra asking Charmain where she thinks Antony is now: "Stands he or sits he? / Or does he walk? Or is he on his horse?" A serio-comic, surrealistic dream sequence follows this clever Shakespearian transposition. Suspended in space, as it were, Sara is united with Murray, who arrives on a horse to kiss her. She strangles him, then rocks him in her arms and wishes for a Keatsian pot of basil to put him in. Peeping from behind a star, she sees two burly policemen with flapping wings as they drop down beside her:

> 'Ah,' said one triumphantly, 'I thought there was something going on here. Dead, is he?'
>
> 'Stone,' said the other laconically, peering down at the man on her breast. 'Blow for the homicide-squad. What did you kill him for lady?'
>
> 'I killed him,' she sobbed, 'because —'
>
> 'I know, I know! You needn't tell me. You killed him because you loved him.'
>
> ' I did not,' she said in the grand manner.   'I killed him because we clicked.'[16]

The reference to Keats's "The Pot of Basil" is appropriate in this passage because the buried head suits the ghoulishness of Duley's sense of humour.

Equally gruesome is the tale of the exploded wife. Having failed to seduce Sara behind a funnel during the Atlantic crossing, the man with the classical nose and bald head recovers his dignity by relating in gory detail how his wife died in 1917 when a ship full of T.N.T. blew up in Bedford Basin, Halifax, Nova Scotia, and how he found her foot after a long search. Sara's ruminations on the kind of foot it may have been are a kind of detached merriment. It is interesting that Hugh MacLennan's *Barometer Rising*, which was published about nine months before *Novelty on Earth*, uses the Halifax disaster as background. If Duley read this book, she saw no reason to excise the exploded wife from her book any more than she hesitated to give the woman who wanted to adopt children the following grisly sentiment: "I'm not in favour of litters. I feel like the man who pined for an hour of Herod." The humour of heartlessness is a distinctive trait of Duley's writing.

The structure of *Novelty on Earth* has the same linear pattern as her other novels. What it lacks is the unity imposed by the cruel birds in *The Eyes of the Gull* and by the capricious sea in *Highway to Valour*. In both of these books the main symbol is an integral part of the themes of escape and endeavour. But in *Novelty on Earth* there is something artificial about the connection, late in the book, between the mysterious child, Christina, and D. H. Lawrence's poem "Gladness of Death." Christina is the memory of Sara Colville's childhood friend who died. Unable to sleep, Christina finds peace only in the "dark sun" of the night, which protects her from the foolishness of her artist-father, who calls his four children after the Pre-Raphaelites, and from her insensitive mother who is "strange, stringy and full of cults." The dead girl becomes the inspiration for the new novel that Sara feels she can finally write after her emotional crisis. Even though Christina's name has occurred often in the story until she is finally identified, she does not fit very well into the novel.

As noted, Christina's "black sun" is based on D. H. Lawrence's 'Gladness of Death,'[17] a poem which Duley uses to illuminate the death of Sara's dreams and the birth of her new hopes. Although Sara cannot predict the future, she knows intuitively that there will be an after-gladness, an after-Murray-life, in the very darkness of which she will feel herself blooming:

> I shall blossom like a dark pansy, and be delighted
> there among the dark sun-rays of death.
> I can feel myself unfolding in the dark sunshine of death
> to something flowery and fulfilled, and with a strange sweet perfume.
>
> D. H. Lawrence: 'Gladness of Death.'

Christina symbolizes Sara's belief about forging a new life before death, as well as a belief in immortality as the "gladness of death" which cannot wither happiness. Although this Christina-Lawrence association is not uninteresting, it is too precious, so that the over-fanciful presentation of Christina's family leads to some overwriting that tends to spoil the ending of the book. Even if the B . . . family, neighbours of the Duley children, who are mentioned in chapter II, are the models for this odd family, the similarity is too tenuous to press.

The secrets of Margaret Duley's life appear to provide the cross-threads of this sophisticated story, while the Lawrence poem serves to reconcile her, as it does Sara, to the deprivations of her existence. If she could not come to full bloom both as artist and woman as loneliness tempered joy, she would perhaps come to fruition in Eternity. But in life Lawrence's beautiful image of the pansy seems to typify Margaret Duley herself, who made wide, graceful gestures and floated about in chiffons and velvets as richly coloured as the perennial flower itself.

There seems little doubt that Duley transfers many of her own problems and experiences to Sara, for her friend Alice Sharples Baldwin supports my speculations about the autobiographical nature of the novel:

> Novelty on Earth was definitely based on an episode of her own life. When the book came out the hero of the story whom she had not heard from since their parting, phoned her long distance. I was greatly impressed and thought it most romantic but she insisted that that chapter was closed now and that she had not been greatly moved by the call.

In addition, Mary Quinn said that Margaret, who was very cross with her for finding the book too wordy, defended it by claiming that it "is a great chunk of living." At the time, Duley's friends assumed that the book was based in part on a sexual relationship of her own; and she herself seemed to indicate something of the kind by writing "It came to this" into her own copy of Novelty on Earth.

Duley's letter to Ellen Elliott in July 1941 provides additional evidence of the autobiographical nature of the novel. Her attitude to men is expressed in the letter with an earthy humour which may have stemmed from a love affair that had concluded unsatisfactorily:

> I agree with you that the seduction of a stimulating male might be better than a course of Vitamin B1 — Truly for women who do not want to be tools of nature — there should be a nice little covey of men roped off & trained in the mental and erotic art — Then when the female had cleared her system she could jingle the keys & the coins in her pocket — & return to the higher life — personally I object to short emotional rations myself — but I also hate to give too much time to it — I adore the comfort of arms — but I find men stupid — & such heavy breathers for the quieter hours.

Alice Sharples Baldwin's speculation concerning Duley's relationship with men is probably as close to the truth as one may come:

> You ask me about her relations with men — I think Margaret's problem here was that she was a Feminine feminist — if I make myself clear? Temperamentally she was a man's woman and a woman of many men. She needed men — could never have been happy without them. But mentally I think she often felt superior to them and resented their assumption of superiority simply because they were male. She had all the hang-ups of today's Women's Libbers but lacked their independence.

Among her beaux were Major Harford Powel[18] and Colonel John McDowell, both of whom were in the American Army and in St. John's during World War Two. The former was a novelist, short story writer and one-time editor of *Collier's*. His fanciful novel *The Virgin Queene* (1928) is an amusing tale of a faked Shakespearian play about Gloriana, and, as well, a compact satire on American and British academic, domestic and journalistic manners. A copy of the work with the author's signature is among the remaining books in Florence Duley's possession.

Since Duley was never communicative about her male friends ("she was too much of a 'gentleman' to mention names," said Alice Baldwin), there is no possibility of identifying the hero of the book with a real person. As Alice Baldwin claims further, the "evidence that *Novelty on Earth* was written 'several years ago' seems to exclude Harford Powel and John McDowell, and the curious must be satisfied with Sara Cobville's sobbing to Murray Blair, 'Yes, you must feel it to write it, and fling it out like an ejection'."

There seems little doubt that if she had found the right man, Duley would have liked to be a wife and mother. In any event, she referred to her writing as the bearing of brain children; and wrote in a gift copy of *Cold Pastoral* "Second brain-child of Margaret Duley." In *Novelty on Earth*, when Margot Hilton says to Sara, "And I suppose your books are a substitute for children?'," she replies: "Brain children, I suppose." Earlier Sara had told Murray "that work is not sufficient for life, neither is the social round that becomes enervating and exhausting. I want something to make, other than books." The painting Sara coveted in a Bond Street gallery reminded her of *Dear Brutus* "and the man who went into the enchanted wood and found his child." The brief scene at the Tate Gallery in London, where she sees "the most achingly beautiful marble of two children with limbs of childlike perfection," is also significant in this regard:

> In a second she had reached it, feeling the lure of rounded legs and arms. She looked hastily around. Was it against the rules to touch? Tentatively she ringed an ankle with her bare hand, feeling the cold of the marble child. She gave the children a pat and walked away, out into the subdued warmth of the afternoon.[19]

It does not necessarily follow from her sensuous longing for children, however, that Duley would have settled easily into marriage and motherhood. It would have required a strong man to live with the tensions that would inevitably be part of a union in which she would expect to have not only a soul-mate but a good deal of independence as well. For all their charm and warmth, both Sara and Margaret Duley have something of the vampire and the militant suffragette about them. As a result, Nora says to Sara: "Sometimes when I see you with men I think you're quite bad. But sometimes when you talk, I think you're more than they want. Men must be ordinary." Duley seems to have been well aware of her own nature.

At this point, it may be useful to make some general remarks about Duley's published works before attempting to discuss the enigmas of her career. It is perhaps unfortunate that she did not publish enough writings to enable one to find any great development in her work. Her creative period was very short and concentrated; for the four novels were written within four years, with the fourth chronologically completed before the third. At its best the style of *The Eyes of the Gull* and of *Cold Pastoral* is as good as that of *Highway to Valour*. The two later books are consistently good because they avoid the weaknesses of the two earlier ones, and have a deeper view of life. In spite of the banal characterization of Peter Keen, one can make a case for *The Eyes of the Gull* being Duley's best book because of its compact structure, single setting and of the fierce symbol of the bird's eyes.

Duley's methods do not change. She avoids complex plots; her stories are linear and are told in the third person narrative and almost exclusively from the woman's point of view. Frequently, she takes the reader into the minds of her characters but there is no real use of the stream of consciousness. The focus, in all the novels, is on the feminine psyche. The male leads are presented with varying degrees of sympathy, a practice not unexpected in an author who likes to cut men down to size. Although she has a strong inclination towards melodrama, this tendency is reduced by good dialogue, original characterization, sharp irony and a hard-hearted sense of comedy. In addition the dialogue between the town characters is cerebral and witty, while that between the outport or rural characters is idiomatic and authentic.

Duley's skill in depicting people is remarkable as she gives a strong sense of the inner and outer lives of her characters while blending very well their physical and psychological traits. Although she deals mostly with adults, she is skilful in her portrayal of children. The baby-talk of games of Rosamund and Jennifer Hervey in *Novelty on Earth* are authentic, as are Patricia Kirke's whims in *Highway to Valour*: "Gimme! It's mine, Moira. Gimme!' is a good example as is a child's announcement, probably overheard from a grown-up, that "Daddy is as drunk as David's sow." Duley's love for animals, as well as for children, is apparent throughout her writing; the presentation of the old dog, Brin, in *Highway to Valour*, for example, is sensitive and moving.

Allusions nourish Duley's natural gift for language. Two random examples will remind the reader of others already noted; while Sara Colville is musing on the difficulties of her love affair, she says, "The Gods knew when to make Lancelot ride by, and it isn't going to be tirra-lirra by the river." When later she takes the decision away from Murray and releases him, "Her voice belonged to a woman who would go, before she was sent to the tents of Shem."

Duley's style is clear and generally unpretentious. She not only has an artist's eye for light and shade as examples of her word-painting have shown, but also she recreates in fine detail the seasons, landscapes, the sea in all its moods, and flowers and trees. All the poetry in her went into her prose; for she was unable to handle verse. As a result, she captured in prose the sights and sounds of Newfoundland: the lilacs and laburnums in late June, the phut-phut of outboard motors on smooth waters, the thud of long-rubbers on beach rocks, the picnic lunches when "the flies appeared to sit on the crumbs," the thunder of surf against granite cliffs and trees stripped of leaves. While Tim Vincent's description of icebergs in *Cold Pastoral*,[20] "I thought I was sailing through a graveyard for Vikings", may strike the reader as less lyrical than the prose poem about icebergs in *Highway to Valour*,[21] Duley's descriptive style remains essentially the same throughout the book. Duley is significant in the literary history of Newfoundland because she wrote truthfully and poetically about a little-known region that she loved more than she hated. In *Novelty on Earth*, Sara Colville told Murray Blair. "I'm never lonely with music. It takes me beyond myself." Newfoundland did much the same for Margaret Duley so that she became one of the most successful and accomplished writers of her time.

1. (10 May 1942), p. 7.
2. (17 May 1942), p. 17.
3. *Novelty on Earth*, (New York, Macmillan, 1942), p. 267. All quotations are from this edition.
4. This remark also suggests that *Novelty on Earth* was written before *Highway to Valour* since the Second World War is declared near the end of the latter.
5. *Novelty on Earth* p. 75.
6. *Ibid.*, p. 96.
7. *Ibid.*, p. 169.
8. *Ibid.*, p. 176.
9. *Ibid.*, p. 177.
10. *Ibid.*, p. 290-91.
11. *Ibid.*, p. 265.
12. *Ibid.*, p. 42-43.
13. *Ibid.* Both the publisner's readers and Duley did not notice the contradiction of having Murray's wife pregnant on p. 7, and then on p. 114 incapable of having any more children. There has been no mention of the miscarriage.
14. *Ibid.* See the restaurant scene in which Margot justifies to Sara and Nora her decision to live with another woman's husband (pp. 239-247).
15. *Ibid.*, p. 9.
16. *Ibid.*, p. 202.
17. *Complete Poems*, ed, Vivian de Sola Pinto & Warren Roberts (New York, The Viking Press, 1941), pp. 676-77.

18. See *Who Was Who Among North American Authors 1921-1931*, Vol. 2 (Detroit, Michigan, Gale Research Company Book Tower, 1976), p. 1167; *Who's Who in American 1950-1951*, Vol. 26 (Chicago, II U.S.A., The A.N. Marquis Company, 1950), p. 2204; and *Who Was Who in America 1951-60*, Vol. 3, p. 696.

19. *Novelty on Earth*, p. 271.

20. p. 178.

21. p. 151. Already quoted.

CHAPTER SEVEN

The Lost Novel

The 1940s were the most productive and successful years of Duley's career and among the most difficult in her personal life. Her two best novels, *Highway to Valour* and *Novelty on Earth*, received more than respectful attention and Macmillan had taken an option on another. In addition, she published *The Caribou Hut* (1949), which is an excellent description of war time St. John's, and wrote at least one very good short story. As a consequence, Marguerite Lovat Dickson predicted at the time that Duley was going "to forge ahead" because she was a writer in the best "Macmillan" tradition who would survive the war and fit herself to the trend of the days to come. Ellen Elliott too saw a great future for her because the Canadian novelist, Mazo de la Roche, was gradually "sliding down the scale as far as Canadian sales are concerned, and I feel her place could be taken by Miss Duley who writes for a woman's audience."

But Duley failed to live up to such great expectations by withdrawing from the literary scene and one wonders why she did so. It has been suggested by Mrs. Kitchell and others that the author was so disillusioned by the reception to her work at home that she came to regard it as "love's labour's lost upon a thankless island." According to this argument, Duley was particularly disturbed "that friends had made light of her work and had inquired as to how she had gained the knowledge [relating to sex] she portrayed in her books." But I very much doubt that she became so sensitive about exposure to the Newfoundland reading public, especially since she had received enough praise from North America and abroad to compensate for slights at home. While she knew that there were some at home who made fun of both herself and her work, therefore, her bruised feelings in this matter cannot be claimed as the main reason that she stopped writing. On the contrary the answer to this mystery is probably to be found in Duley's personal life at the time.

Cyril Duley's letter to Gladys on 20 November 1940 in which he discusses their mother's death and will refers to the strain of the whole affair on Margaret. She was so tense at the time that Cyril felt "something must be done for her and accordingly I am going to get her away on a trip to Montreal and Toronto within the next few days. It's going to be a bit of a financial strain on me, but I really think it is due her and my duty to make it possible." Apart from the let down for her at the end of this traumatic period, Margaret was also anxious about the manuscript of *Highway to Valour* which she had recently sent off to Macmillan.

Having arrived in Montreal by the end of November, she decided to go to New York to see her literary agent, after which she spent Christmas and New Years with Gladys in Winston-Salem. In February she went to Toronto, where she met Ellen Elliott for the first time, then to Montreal again; and finally she returned to St. John's. This approximately five-month trip did her a great deal of good although her changing moods still indicated that there might be trouble ahead.

On 12 March 1941 she was in buoyant spirits as she wrote to Ellen Elliott from Montreal that she had just lunched with Leo Cox the poet ("really an interesting intellectual is Leo, if he would take off the seven veils instead of putting them on") and that she would be dining with Mrs. Lovat Dickson the next day: "I find her particularly interesting about Mrs. Eayrs and Grey Owl & all that marvellously vital galere." Hugh Eayrs was president of the Canadian Macmillan Company, while Grey Owl was the Englishman who pretended to be a North American Indian and whose work as a wild life author was published by H. Lovat Dickson of the London Macmillan Company. Such remarks indicate that Duley enjoyed the literary chitchat associated with being a well known writer herself. Meanwhile, she informs Ellen Elliot in her letter that she was planning to return to Newfoundland shortly because it was time she picked up "routine and everydayness":

My brain is intrigued with a novel — but nothing will clarify as yet — & I feel I am waiting to get off the shifting sand — The sea-motif is always with me — 'rise with my rising — with thee subside' but once I cast an anchor I may shift less restlessly & begin Scorpion Grass.

Another faint clue to the contents of the novel that Duley mentions here appears in a letter from Ellen Elliott to Marguerite Lovat Dickson on 13 March 1941: "A new novel [by Margaret Duley] is taking shape and it is a blend of the other two — worldliness and simplicity." Margaret later told a Toronto reporter that the book was about the Second World War.

A few days after her letter to Ellen Elliott, Duley wrote to her again in a less cheerful mood, perhaps because she was dreading the crossing of the Cabot Strait, the ninety-mile stretch of water between Nova Scotia and Newfoundland, which at the time was a hunting ground for the German U-boats in the North Atlantic. In fact, her fears about this voyage were verified when the *S.S. Caribou*, the boat on which she travelled, was later torpedoed on 4 October 1942 with the loss of 137 people. At the time of her journey, then, the war was obviously on her mind; and perhaps her broken romance was too. She even seemed to feel guilty about enjoying herself, as she continues in her letter to make remarks about "eating the flesh of fat bullocks" and about "the fleshpots of Egypt":

> What a sad mad bloodsome business it all is — I could be like Shelley &
> 'lie down like the tired child' but I know I must say Excelsior — & go out
> & let a man I don't care in the least about, give me food and drink — a
> lesser woman than yourself told me my feet were always in puddles — &
> that I cried perpetually in my heart — I have a feeling I should join the
> Salvation Army and be truly shriven.

Duley's triumph in the success of *Highway to Valour* was wearing off, while, at the same time, she knew that to return home was to relive her mother's last illness as well as to watch Nelson go steadily downhill. In addition, it was difficult for her to cope with the complexities of publishing two books almost simultaneously while trying to write another. The old order at home was changing with the collapse of the family business and Cyril's decision to marry.

By June 1941 the new book had been given the title of *The Hollow and the Crest* when Duley wrote Miss Pindyck in New York that she hoped it would be finished by the late autumn. But she did not seem to be able to work consistently at it so that the manuscript did not reach the readers at Macmillan until 7 January 1944, by which time the title had been changed to *Octaves of Dawn*. The manuscript, which was returned to Duley in Winston-Salem on 19 February 1944, has not survived and Ellen Elliott's correspondence about it is not available. Why the book was rejected is therefore conjectural. Perhaps Duley refused to make the revisions that the readers at Macmillan may have suggested; perhaps the manuscript was rejected outright. Whatever the case, there is evidence that Duley probably burned the work in disgust. In a letter to Ellen Elliott in September 1941, she explained her request for another copy of a review from an Ottawa paper that she had lost by blaming it on her "passion for burning up the past." This remark about burning probably accounts also for the fact that not a single manuscript of Duley's work has been found.

The continuing correspondence between Ellen Elliott and Duley provides hints that there may have been other reasons for Duley's difficulties with writing at this time. For Duley, spring in Newfoundland was a dismal time, when physical strength was at a low ebb, and the long wait for summer a trial to her soul. She had been home for more than two months and seemed haunted by thoughts of her mother. She had gone away so quickly after the funeral that perhaps only now was grief catching up with her as well as those vague feelings of guilt that often occur after the death of a parent. Since she had dabbled in spiritualism with Ellen Elliott in Toronto, she now appeared to desire contact with her mother's spirit. Although there is no record of Duley's letter to her, Ellen Elliott replied on 22 May 1941 to what was certainly a request for help of a psychical nature:

> I will do my best to get in touch with your friend, and if I do I shall, of
> course, let you know all about it. But in the meantime, cut out the grief.
> Not only are you damaging yourself but you are doing her a great deal
> of harm — and anyway (I know I sound terribly callous) death isn't so
> terrible. From what I can discover, my dead friends have a damned

sight better time than I do. But seriously, don't worry about her; your first contact with the next world which you made when you were here will have far wider reaching results than any of us can understand at the moment, and if you can do without the grieving you will probably be making your own contact with her anyway.

Marguerite Lovat Dickson thought that the "friend" mentioned here was probably Margaret's mother. Ellen Elliott had asked Dickson on 10 March 1941 if Duley had spoken of "our talks, and of one very strange thing that happened while she was here, but if not I will when I see you. It is much too long to write about and it would be much too difficult." The "strange thing" probably happened at a séance which, according to Dickson, was "put on" for Margaret when she was in Toronto in February. Perhaps Ellen Elliott overestimated the importance of this occult experience for her friend, for Duley was certainly somewhat disingenuous about the whole affair, probably because she did not want to offend her friend. At any rate, Dickson's recollection of the séance is probably as close to the truth of the matter as one is likely to come:

But I cannot remember E. E. reporting anything outstanding. Margaret disparaged the séance to me, saying that the medium was an under-nourished pathetic girl of fifteen and that the surroundings were depressing if not seedy. She would have said this to Ellen. The 'friend' was her mother? Not her fiancé?

Dickson's reference to a fiancé is unexplained.

Since Ellen Elliott is dead and her papers destroyed, there is not much to go on. She appears, however, to have been associated with Mackenzie King's interest in the occult. Canadian historian C. P. Stacey wrote to me on 30 October 1978 that the Prime Minister attended a séance with Elliott at her apartment on Heath Street in Toronto on 5 August 1942:

Whether King had other contacts with Ellen Elliott I don't know; but his diary entry for 5 August 1942 says that on meeting her at the Macmillan office he was greatly surprised at the extent of her interest in psychical phenomena. It is possible that this is the only séance he had with her.[1]

It is difficult to say how deeply Duley was involved in spiritualism. One suspects, however, that her interest was not very deep and that in1941 it became for her a fortification against emotional stress.

The summer weather did not revive her. Tired and frayed, she wrote to Ellen Elliott in August that she felt "like a Hell-cat over galleys — blurbs for jackets — & publicity questions — & family interference — and mentally & spiritually I am as comfortable as a hair shirt — and also immensely irritated at all the people who will expect to receive an autographed copy of *Highway*." In her letter, she shows her depression over the war as well as her truculent humour concerning men. Consequently, she refers to her remarks in an earlier letter of the need to have a covey of men roped off for use like Vitamin B1 when needed, and thereby demonstrates that she was obviously feeling unfulfilled in her personal life in spite of her ribald tone:

Yes, St. John's — is interesting *if* you like the pound of lorries — the tread of army boots — & men around with faces full of past & present. Full of wives — They all look so buttoned up — when you know it is a disguise for the male animal — & how can you expect them to behave like a horse-hair sofa, when the lower instincts are being trained & intensified — Military men have no minds — naval men are all wet — flying men are too high — So what? The perfect feminine life should comprise a stalwart wellwashed policeman at the front gate — on guard — a philosopher or two — remote & exalted in the attic to absorb one's sense of higher thought — and then one might want to be a tool of nature — so imagine the conflict over policeman and philosopher.

The times were out of joint for her in every way, and significantly she makes no mention of *Octaves of Dawn*. The publication and reception of *Highway to Valour* in September cheered her, however, and her childlike delight over the reviews was refreshingly free from conceit. In October she was laid low with a bout of lumbago. Because she felt "cast up like a scooped out shell on the wet line of the beach," she wrote to Ellen Elliott: "If I hadn't built Margaret up to be such a brave *gal* I'd have a good cry — but I feel I have to keep rowing the boat to get her to Labrador & I'm not in the mood to cry 'Excelsior' or what have you." But she was very upset, nevertheless, that she had done no work for a month. When the lumbago cleared up, her temperature soared and she took to her bed with doses of sulfanilamide. At this time, she writes, a Colonel "came to town & insisted on seeing me with anything but a bedside manner — so-what? I am retabli — but trying to marry off my brother — & pull up some roots that shriek like mandrakes." The colonel was possibly John McDowell who in July had been referred to by Duley as a grammarian who corrected the "wafty" syntax of the proofs of *Highway to Valour* in accordance with the best traditions of American English. Cynical about men, and not very interested in the colonel, Duley was looking forward to visiting the Barbizon Plaza in New York in November to see about *Novelty on Earth*, to have cocktails with the editor of *American Magazine*, and to do anything except concentrate on her new novel.

Meanwhile, her fan mail was accumulating. A man even wrote to ask how to transport his car from Canada to Newfoundland; and Duley was typically amused: "He appears to be afraid of the tidal wave." In a flurry of pre-journey excitement, she rushed around "like Mad Ophelia," preparing a radio talk and expecting her voice to be "like the death-rattle." About this time also, she claimed that she had written "a very sophisticated short story — but it is much too smart, I know, for the masses — & much too shock-making to tradition." But no such story has come to light. Although her spirits seem to have lifted, her thoughts and her actions were too scattered for sustained literary composition; so *Octaves of Dawn* simply marked time.

When she came home in March 1941 from the trip after their mother's death, she soon realized that Cyril would marry Florence Pitcher. Although she was happy for him, his marriage tended to emphasize her spinsterhood, so that, in spite of Florence's generous disposition, Duley would have to play second fiddle to the wife of a brother who had always been her good companion. As soon as the wedding was over, she travelled to New York to meet with the editor of *American Magazine*. She had anticipated this trip with pleasure as she implied in a letter to Ellen Elliott: "... If I am not writing at least I will be drinking in New York." Beneath the cheerfulness and the wit of her letters at' this time there was a sense of loss which she probably thought new surroundings would cure. Thus she went the usual rounds of New York, Winston-Salem, Toronto, and Montreal, sometimes staying for brief periods with friends, but more often living in small residential hotels where she would write and maintain the privacy that she liked.

Having left home during the week of 5 November 1941 when Florence and Cyril were married, Duley did not return until June 1942, nearly six months after Nelson's death on 15 January 1942. Although few details of this trip have been recorded, she seems to have been in Toronto in the spring when *Novelty on Earth* appeared in the bookstores. An article entitled "A Visiting Author" in the Toronto *Evening Telegram* not only indicates her presence in the city at this time but also gives an indication of her literary reputation:

> She writes books as easily as most women spring houseclean, and almost as quickly ... Next came *Novelty on Earth* ... which arrived on the bookshelves this week, and lastly there's the as yet unfinished novel which Miss Duley is working on now and expects to have finished within the next thirty days ... Obviously the author is a prolific writer. She is also an omnivorous reader and a loquacious talker! ... 'I collect human impressions instead of knickknacks,' she explained, 'and they don't have to be dusted all the time. I write them out in longhand, then put them through the typewriter until my book is finished.' ... Miss Duley is a dark, gracious, vital woman — keen about her work and her native heath, Newfoundland. She likes people and solitude, and is an enthusiastic woman-booster. She says war has proved woman's ability outside the home, and she hopes women never return to the inane life of prewar. She's all for the career wife.[2]

She was in fine fettle on the day that she gave that interview, in spite of her equivocating over her dalliance with *Octaves of Dawn*. If her complaints to Ellen Elliott meant anything, she was *not* getting on with it, and *The Telegram's* month stretched to more than a year and a half. Although the sequence of events between November 1941 and June 1942 is obscure, it does help to some extent to explain Duley's literary paralysis. When she left for New York, T. J. Duley and Company no longer existed, for the firm had been forced out of business because it could not compete with larger stores that were selling large quantities of the newly popular costume jewellery, and because Nelson was in no condition to help Cyril keep the firm solvent. After this, Mrs. Duley became ill, Nelson was a worry and Cyril was showing the effects of having borne the brunt of winding things up. It was not a cheeful household; and while Margaret was away, Nelson died in January 1942, in Pool's Cove, Fortune Bay, where he was buried. There was no point in her coming home to try to reach that out-of-the-way place in time for his funeral.

Meanwhile, *Novelty on Earth* was published in April 1942; and the author basked in the sunshine of its reception, with the telephone call from her old flame probably stirring her in spite of her avowed indifference. The settling of the Duley Company's affairs and Nelson's estate caused friction in the family as some letters of the time indicate. Margaret's letter to Gladys, for example, which was written sometime in June 1942 from the Westminster Hotel in Toronto, shows how much she prized her privacy when away from home. Being unable to book a seat on the first Trans-Canada Air Lines commercial plane to arrive at Torbay Airport on 1 May 1942, Margaret writes that she will travel to Newfoundland by train and "the crawling Caribou which journey is as pleasing to me as the exodus of the children of Israel." She was reluctant to leave the Westminster Hotel, however, for there she had found for the first time "reasonable quarters and a truly magnificent room and both for twelve fifty a week and a most reasonable dining room to eat in." She was obviously cross at having to leave the hotel and even more angry at Cyril for wanting her to take part in the discussions with Mr. Ingpen of the Royal Trust Company,who was handling the disposition of the estate.

In this matter, Margaret played the role of the queen of tragedy to the hilt as she emphasized her "gigantic bombing," which had brought Cyril to his senses. This phrase seems to indicate also Margaret's own trials and tribulations, as well as the sorry story of Nelson's life and the wrangling over the disposition of what was left of their patrimony. As a consequence, she announces in her letter to Gladys that she felt like a piece of tissue-paper which someone had crushed into a ball and thrown into the corner: "It has done terrible violence to my nature — *but now that my writing capacity has been completely destroyed* [my italics] and I have to gather some strength I have decided to face it and go home — but I am writing to say if there is the slightest raised voice or discussion I will go to the hospital and function from my bed."

In her next letter to Gladys, which was written five days after her return to St. John's, Margaret dropped the histrionics and said she was given a fine welcome, adding that "by my disarming attitude everything moved along very well." The house was all freshened up with new colours and drapes; and Margaret was charmed with Cyril's wife: "Florence is truly a genuinely good girl." Florence later lived up to this assessment, for Margaret lived with her and Cyril, whenever she was home, until 1944 when the couple moved to the house at 7 Monkstown Road, which had been left to Cyril by Lionel Chancey.

Meanwhile, Margaret was worrying about her writing as well as another troublesome matter about which she sought advice from Mr. Ingpen as she informed Gladys: "& my position worsens, — I find I am an alien in U.S. — & now an alien in Nfld. unless I spend six months here — I asked Ingpen if there was anything I could do at present & he said no — My greatest distress is the interruption in my work. I seem to be in a mental non-creative desert — & I cannot think of a thing to say." Two days later, however, her situation had improved a little: "Last night thank God, I wrote one or two feeble words professionally — & this morning I was able to manage forty or fifty."

When the legal transaction of the estate was nearing completion, Margaret planned to return to Canada at the end of September. She had calmed down considerably, seemed to enjoy Mr. MacDermott's visit (he stayed for three years at Florence's invitation because he was "such a sweet old thing and Cyril enjoyed his company") and she loved seeing "Dicky" again ("Florence does not mind his feet on the new spread").

Two weeks after she arrived home, Margaret decided to make her will because she felt she should make a fresh start in an organized way. As she wrote to Gladys, she wanted at her death to be disposed of "with dispatch and simplicity and to be cremated if I am where I can be cremated, and to have my ashes buried as I do not wish to stand around on the shelf. If I am where there is only the earth I accept that as I do not wish to take a ride in the baggage coach ahead." The making of her will also caused her to consider her assets such as the English contract with Methuen for *Highway to Valour* and their option on *Novelty on Earth*, which was later published as *Green Afternoon* in 1944. The only financial hitch was the fact that "such sums in pounds will not be able to be used until the war is over." On the other hand, as Mr. Ingpen informed her, the Duley estate was larger than had been anticipated.

Meanwhile, Margaret had regained all her old fondness for Cyril who, she now realized, had borne the weight of his brother's excesses, and who in the bad years of the business had not only paid the shop assistants their salaries out of his own pocket but also had directed that his sisters be given the monthly amounts willed to them. Consequently, Margaret becomes more tolerant of the family as she learns more about the business: "there is much complication other than the lobster fishing. As a family, and with the knowledge that none of us can ever be quite independent of the group, we must all accept a part in Nelson's failure, which I trust is only a lower body failure as he was never vicious in the least." Since Margaret and Gladys often used cryptical phrases or pseudonyms to discuss matters and people, "the lobster fishery" in the letter probably refers to the mess Nelson had helped to create for the business and himself, or perhaps it indicates conflicts in the living arrangements at home. In this case, Margaret could perhaps be excused for wanting to be off again because "in the house I am always conscious of Nelson's feet and Mother's sunken figure." It is interesting to note that Margaret's letters to Gladys at this time contain several examples of the codes that they often used. Describing the trip home, its long waits and the inconveniences that made "Siberia seem more accessible", for example Margaret gives the impression that she was receiving unwelcome attentions from a young man:

> Albert intruded several times, and he has been here in person. He was also in evidence at certain times on the journey & for one whole night I thought of nothing else. He is a sinister young man & there were times he made my life as bleak as Egypt. I thought I could get rid of him for a while, — I did on the train, but he called at the house, & for a while we

have to endure him as a guest. Cyril & Florence are very good about him.

Since Florence does not remember a sinister young man called Albert, he is probably an emblem for Margaret's fears about her future, or for fits of depression over unrequited love. Similarly, in a letter ten days later, she writes again of this enigmatic young man:

> . . . I have been home two weeks — Alfred has changed so much of living that it feels like another world, and since the intrusion of that materialistic gentleman, coming home is like returning to some strange Klondike where many things run riot. It is an odd commentary, that to accept Alfred's guardianship, we have to be protected against Alfred.

Alfred may, of course, be Ingpen, or he may represent the involved money matters themselves. Such epistolary puzzles are worth mentioning because they reflect Margaret's secrecy and her love of mental games.

One can only speculate about Margaret's activities on her return to Canada. She probably worked on *Octaves of Dawn* at the Westminster Hotel, where the manager had allowed her to leave her heavy luggage since the preceding June 1942. But what delayed the completion of the book until January 1944? The best explanation seems to be that she had written herself out, or was simply tired of publishers' politics. At any rate, sickness, deaths and financial upheavals in the family, her sexual frustrations, and the unbelievable recurrence of war with its added horror of Hitler's genocide, seem to have overwhelmed her.

Although the writing of *Highway to Valour* and *Novelty on Earth* had lifted her spirits somewhat, they could not maintain for her the emotional balance she had gained after their success; and so she suffered a loss of creativity. Freedom from worry about money (she had made rather lavish bequests in the draft of her will that she had shown to Mr. Ingpen) and the clearing up of her misunderstanding with Cyril did not seem to help her to reorganize her life; and, as a consquence, her writing faded into the background.

The different titles of Duley's last novel, *Scorpion Grass, The Hollow and The Crest* and *Octaves of Dawn*, have theosophical overtones that seem to support the opinions of friends who thought that her "isms" were responsible for its rejection by the publisher. Alice Sharples Baldwin felt certain that the book was "devoted to expounding those ideas to the detriment of the story. I remember thinking so when she read me excerpts. I think it was a great disappointment to her and I think . . . [its rejection] put her off further writing." The final title, *Octaves of Dawn*, was probably taken from E. J. Pratt's poem "Newfoundland".

> Here the winds blow . . .
> They call with the silver fifes of the sea . . .
> They are one with the tides of the sea
> They are one with the tides of the heart,
> They blow with the rising octaves of dawn,
> They die with the largo of dusk . . .

This passage recalls Margaret's assertion to Ellen Elliott that "The sea motif is always with me" and further suggests that the novel was probably not as esoteric as Mrs. Baldwin remembered. More likely, it was not up to the mark of originality required by Macmillan.

In view of the foregoing speculations, one may draw some tentative conclusions concerning Duley's lost novel. Among her literary remains are twenty typewritten sheets (pp. 220-240), three quarters of a sheet (p. 141) and two snipped-off pieces of paper, all of which seem to be parts of *Octaves of Dawn*. These passages deal largely with the attempt of Juliana Brooking to save an old woman who suffocates in a fire, the girl's mental and physical hurts and her decision to leave Newfoundland to marry Alex Graham ("the imported artist for John Cabot and his son Sebastian") when his divorce is final. As a result, Juliana sells the land on which the mansion ("Burst Heart Hill") has stood to Hugh Jennings, who is described as "the death and glory boy" and, who loses "the town's most exclusive girl" to another man. Juliana, who is the last of the Brookings, retains her shares in the family shipping company because she may some day have a son who "would like to do business in great waters."

The setting of these literary fragments is obviously St. John's and the events in them revolve around a great mercantile family who lost their house and their famous Auk's Egg (not explained in the twenty-page remnant) in the fire of '92, but saved their wharf-business. "They built again though what they built shocked the square edged city of St. John's." Later the house is razed to the ground. Mr. Boyd, the President of the company, emerges as a father figure, who seems to be a combination of Mr. Duley and Mr. Ingpen, the latter having become "dear Ink" by the time Margaret Duley had finished her consultations with him in 1942: ". . . he is truly a lamb of a man . . . His quality is superb, soothing and impeccable and I should like him for a father in my next incarnation." There are also in the fragments Susan Wilking, who blames herself for starting the fire, her husband Jeff, a man called Jacob who is a butler or a handyman, a matriarchal grandmother who dies earlier in the draft, a grandfather who walks wildly up Burst Heart Hill "when he received the official wire saying his sons and nephews were dead," Mary Ann, a bed-ridden, difficult servant who smothers in the smoke and a woman called Henri's wife who has no toenails and who was probably tortured in the war.

Although this fragment is frustratingly brief, it does show not only that Duley wanted to keep the Newfoundlnd scene at the centre of her writing, but also that she could no longer write as well as previously. As a result, the events that she describes are sensational, lachrymose and redundant. Perhaps the uneven style of the passage springs from a compulsion to express vicariously the personal sorrows that the author has rigorously suppressed outside her books, or until now has transmogrified within them. In this light, both Juliana's thoughts and words are similar to Margaret's confidences to Ellen Elliott in the letters of 1941, as well as in those to her Somerset relatives in the fifties: "In a hospital bed Juliana Brooking lay stranded on a lee-shore"; "It's not us, Sue . . . We're just figures in the pattern"; and "They are actors for all events that bring change, Sue, Nana always said we could not have had the Christian story without Judas — she would never let me see him contemptibly — she said in some patterns there were the hard parts to play — necessary parts." In *Highway to Valour*, Duley deals with "the agony of living" with lyric dignity; but in these examples there is no such sublimation:

> She felt she was learning the pain of creation, the throb of the seed as it broke thorugh the earth, the gasp of the fish leaving the sea, the fall of the high-winged bird, the totter of the soldier taken in battle. She saw the wandering of homeless animals, the excessive spawn of the sea and the earth. She thought of cruelty, of the fair passing of her grandmother and the suffocating of Mary Ann. She thought of the travail of ships and the waters rushed over her head.

This is old wine in a new bottle. Duley has said it all before, and much better, in *Highway to Valour*. Always sensitive to the problem of pain, she here is inclined to sermonize about it, instead of transforming it into something more splendid. One cannot prove that this extract was written after *Highway to Valour*, or that it is the ending of *Octaves of Dawn*; and there is the possibility that these pages of typescript are part of the "bad book" which Duley said she had torn up several years earlier. But there are certain similarities between the author's life and the fragment which suggest that it is likely to be part of *Octaves of Dawn*. The resemblance between Mr. Boyd and Mr. Ingpen, for instance, seems more then coincidental; while Mary Ann's death is messy in a way that reminds one of Nelson's declining years. In addition, the emphasis in the fragment on the sea and ships and on the nature of Julian's musing about being "locked up in the mystery of living" seems to place it in the 1940s as the author knew them.

---

1. See C. P. Stacey, *A Very Double Life: The Private World of Mackenzie King* (Toronto, Macmillan of Canada; 1976), pp. 196-97 for reference to séance.

2. (13 May 1942), p. 9

CHAPTER EIGHT

The Short Stories and The Caribou Hut

Duley once told her niece, Margot Duley Morrow, that a good short story is "the presentation of an ordinary, and even banal event in unusual circumstance or surrounding." By adhering as much as possible to this advice in her own short stories, Duley produced a couple of stories which are so skillful and perceptive that one wishes she had written more of them. There is no doubt that the author herself was very pleased with one or two of her stories as she indicated after her best story, "Mother Boggan", was published in England in *The Fortnightly* for April 1940.[1] Later, when she was informed by G. E. Rogers that Macmillan was interested in *Highway to Valour*, she responded by telling him that, in spite of the fact that she had already published two novels and a story or two in London, her "largest prestige was *The Fortnightly* — between Dean Inge and Dorothy Sayers." Another indication of the quality of her story in *The Fortnightly* is the fact that a year later the wife of H. Lovat Dickson, the part-owner and director of the periodical (from 1929 to 1932), was to become her friend.

The story is a controlled, dramatic yarn, which is set in a Newfoundland outport, and which focuses on the tall rocks resembling human forms that stand in many bays along the coast. Specifically, it is a purgative, bucolic story about slack-jawed Joel O'Toole and two such rocks: Mad Moll "crouching in front . . . Snaky and slimy with sea-weed hair . . . [and slobbering] all day with the water going over her head'; and Mother Boggan which is clean, stout and maternal with her granite cape reddened by the sunset. The author gives a new twist to the motif of the village idiot by making a rock a mother-figure for Joel, the slouching, unattractive, forty-year old imbecile whom none of the girls will marry. Until her death, his mother does his thinking for him; later he goes to war in 1914 and finds a substitute mother in the army because it tells him what to do and when to do it.

In the story, Duley uses this connection between the idiot's mother and his wartime protector, the army, to achieve some remarkable effects. "At Beaumont Hamel where Newfoundlanders fell like ninepins . . . [Joel] couldn't be killed" because his mother kept stepping between him and his fallen companions and calling to him to protect him from danger. Thus she returns from the grave to nurture her simple-minded son's craving for her protection. In this way, Duley achieves a fine balance between hallucination and realism which gives the story a fine spectral impact.

When Joel returns from France after the war, his land, house and war pension make him rich enough to be a good catch for the daughters of the shore. Although their mothers think that their daughters could do worse than marry him, the girls cannot bear his foolish guffaws and sagging mouth. Poor Joel feels lonelier than ever after each of his frequent proposals is refused. Heavy-hearted, he rows his yellow dory alongside Mother Boggan to "talk his heart out to the woman in the granite cape." In a sense, the huge rock "belonged to Joel," but to the rest of the village "she were a nasty bit of rock to run the skiff up agin." For many years, however, Joel cannot find "the sanctuary of direction," even though his spectral mother continues to protect him as when she calls to him and saves him from a falling tree that had been dislodged by lightning. Finally, he becomes despondent when young Annie, who has considered marrying him to help out her needy family, goes into domestic service instead. In utter desolation, Joel rows out to seek comfort from his granite mother. Trying to lay his face against her bosom, which is wet and slippery after twelve days of rain, he capsizes his dory and drowns under her swishing skirts, grinning happily as he hears his Mother's voice calling, "Joel, come here! Joel, come here!" Perhaps the capitalization of "Mother" in the last paragraph of the story is an attempt by the author to evoke by analogy the Blessed Virgin as a mother who takes her child away from misery and pain. Duley was certainly aware that in many a Newfoundland outport the Mother of God is represented not only as a statue in a church or home and in place-names like Conception Bay and Maryvale and Christian names like Mary Immaculate and Madonna, but also as a kind of living presence as Mother Boggan seems to be to Joel.

"Mother Boggan" is a story of uncompromising vision which is tinged with the combined sense of pity and revulsion that an odd man out so often evokes:

> 'Giv us a kiss, Annie?' That would tell. If she could kiss him without dying she could marry him! She closed her eyes on the lily-pond, and the kiss from the sagging mouth smacked from her chin to her nose leaving a wet horror. Her flesh crawled and she flung her people to the dole. Her eyes woke on the lily-pond and she knew the nature of defilement. She ran through the alders.[2]

Joel misreads Annie's promise to give him an answer the next night as an acceptance. As a result, he "grinned at the lilies. He was going to be married, he was going to be married." After he realizes his error, death becomes the only cure for his pain.

The grim drama of "Mother Boggan" is ironically underscored by Duley's pictures of a beautiful, quiet countryside that are presented with splendid colour and precision. In this way, Duley describes Timothy hay, the sun shining red on Mother Boggan, meadowland, potato-patches, reeds waving in ponds in long lines of purple and green to shade the water-lilies, whose white petals are "flung open falling away from golden hearts" to reveal "piercing yellow and waxen white . . . heart shaped leaves." Similarly, in wintertime, Mother Boggan is described in a cloak of gleaming ice, the fish stages and spruce trees are sharply etched against the bleak horizon, while Joel's house is reflected in the waters of the arm which in the shade

> was deep ebony, turning iridescent where it held a sunset and an upside down world.
> Walking so far Joel turned to look. Chewing his cud of hay he yearned towards the world under the water. There was the sharp lines of the hills, a green boat keel to keel and his own house with its bright red door joining the other in the meadow. It made him feel richer to see his two homes. Some day he would enter his house through the high polish of the black water.[3]

Duley's unpublished "Granny Goes the Last Mile" is another short story which focusses on the grim aspects of life and death in a Newfoundland outport.[4] The narrator of the story tells abut a funeral that she and her friend see in one of the more remote corners of Newfoundland. The cortège comes from another settlement because the young girl in the coffin had expressed a wish to be buried beside her mother. The long line of hot and dusty mourners trudges to the cemetery "high up on a hill; necessarily arduous of approach because of the scarcity of earth too near the sea."

> On either side of a dejected white pony walked two men with grizzled faces under crepe wreathed caps, with streamers falling far below their waists. Each carried an impromptu pole from which fluttered a flimsy Union Jack. The pony strained against its harness and the weight of the cart inadequate of accommodation for the full length of the coffin. A bit protruding over the back trailed wisps of material from a pall of indefinite pink, which looked as if a curtain had been dragged from a pole to do some mournful duty.

The narrator and her friend, who are city dwellers, are struck by the sight of Mrs. O'Toole,

> an old crone sitting astraddle the pink-palled coffin, her skinny legs making uncomfortable emergence from a rusty black coat, as she rocked backwards and forwards beating the foot of the coffin with wrinkled old hands.

The mournful sounds of the old woman's keening are appropriately accompanied by "the scrape of wheels, the scuff of tired feet [and] the rising and subsiding of the North Atlantic." Mrs. O'Toole, with her "red rheumy eyes, toothless mouth, and the crepe hat askew on disturbed grey hair" seems an extraordinary sight to the city girls.

Full of curiosity about this startling ritual of mourning, the narrator learns that old Mrs. O'Toole has been caring for her orphaned granddaughter and her five brothers and sisters. When the girl realizes she is dying, she is terrified and pleads with her granny to go with her in death. The old woman tells the demented child that she cannot leave the others to fend for themselves, but she does promise to go to the grave-yard with her. When the narrator asks whether it is necessary for the old woman to ride on top of the coffin, she is told that Mrs. O'Toole can travel the six-mile journey only in this way because she is "gone in the legs" and there is only one horse and cart in the cove. At the same time, the outport woman, who thus answers the arrogant "townie", concludes by roundly comdemning the Health Officers who came round "with the freezin' cure," opened all the nailed-down windows and thereby killed poor Wilmot. In this way, the tensions between the local people and outsiders are put to effective use in Duley's story. As a result, the strength of the work is its lack of sentimentality; while its weaknesses include an ill-judged touch of humour near the end and some turgid sentences; "A cart inadequate of accommodation for the full length of the coffin," for example, is a clumsy way to say that something is too short, while the description of Mrs. O'Toole's "skinny legs making uncomfortable emergence from a rusty black coat" shows a similar ineptness of expression. Such unevenness of writing undoubtedly explains the rejection of "Granny Goes the Last Mile" by *The Atlantic Monthly*; but one is curious, nevertheless, as to why Duley did not revise the story.

Perhaps the fact that Duley published very few short stories is explained by her unwillingness to accede to requests for revisions to her work. Alice Sharples Baldwin believed this to be the case:

> She had difficulty placing short stories because she had no disposition to follow rules and regulations, nor to consider the market she was writing for. I remember her exclaiming furiously — 'They say it's an excellent story but it's not in keeping with their Editorial Policy, *Who cares* about their stupid old editorial policy?' Needless to say this attitude did not smooth the way for her. But I greatly respected it. She was not interested as so many young writers are in learning the tricks of the trade, she wrote as she felt and as she thought best. After a set-to with an Editor she would often remark with a merry glint in her eye — 'I may be writing for posterity,' — but she was not writing for the present Editor of this or that magazine. She took her work very seriously — I should say she was both disciplined and dedicated — she would often say to me, 'No, no, don't do that, your work will suffer'. . . I'm afraid I did not give my work the priority that she gave hers.

Mrs. Baldwin's remark about discipline and dedication needs qualification in view of Margaret's failure to get *Octaves of Dawn* published or to make an effort to rework the potentially excellent "Granny Goes the Last Mile." The editor of the *American Magazine* wanted something from her; while another friend said she wrote a story for *Colliers*. But an exhaustive search of periodicals has revealed only two published stories, "Mother Boggan" and three years later "Sea Dust" which appeared in the November 1943 issue of *Chatelaine*.[5]

"Sea Dust" is about a young sailor named Scott who risks his life to rescue a black cat. The cat is a "Dutch" deserter from the British, who had been Scott's mascot at the evacuation of Dunkirk and Brest, and who had been aboard a ship that was torpedoed off the coast of Newfoundland. After a stay in the hospital in St. John's, Scott returns to duty and is killed, while Jet, the indestructible cat, remains with Eve, the upper-class canteen girl, and has kittens by "a Newfoundland gentleman." Similarly, the story ends happily when Eve's fiancé returns home to her. In many ways, "Sea Dust" is a fine short story: its structure is firm, its prose balanced and clear, while its presentation of its setting in St. John's is vivid and authentic. It is particularly fine in its evocation of the wartime atmosphere of the hostel named the "Caribou Hut". In addition, one is impressed by such descriptions as the black cat licking an ice cream cone with a drunken sailor as well as by the haunting image of boys becoming seadust. But the story lacks, nevertheless, the fine tone and atmosphere of the two outport stories.

I have been able to discover only three other short stories by Duley, "The International Tramp", "Tender Is the Night" and "Age Cannot Dither Her"; all of these unpublished stories appear to have been written from 1953 to 1965.[6] In subject matter, these stories reflect Duley's recent travels in Europe and the more familiar setting of Newfoundland, as well as the more fanciful setting of the far North. Consequently, the stories contain references to Capri, Camellias in Sorrento and St. Mark's Cathedral in Venice, as well as to the electronic Distant Early Warning System (the D.E.W. line) north of Frobisher Bay, which was designed to protect the western hemisphere from an attack by Russia, and to a hero who is a veteran of the Korean War. Such evidence from the stories themselves indicates that they are works of the 1950s; and, in addition, the quality of their composition sheds light on the decline of Duley's creative powers as a writer. In a word, it seems that at this time she was encountering increasing difficulty in sustaining herself as a writer even in the short story, which is a much less demanding genre than the novel. The stories are therefore important to a full understanding of the author.

"The International Tramp" is a hum-drum rather illogical story about an estranged husband and wife who are reunited at the wedding of a friend. Lisa had left Fitz because he had been too wrapped up in his work as an electrical and mechanical engineer, which took him all over the world to test thermal noise, or "solve construction problems in the permafrost"; and, to make matters worse, when he was at home, he would come to dinner after the roast was ruined and the lettuce wilted. Fitz is asked to work on the DEW Line for three years; and Lisa agrees to go with him because she is certain that he will have nowhere to roam in the solitude of the Arctic region. Thus she hopes that he will always have to come home. The quality of this story, which is much like the regular fare in *Good Housekeeping* and *Ladies' Home Journal*, may indicate a further deterioration in Duley's ability to write or perhaps an attempt to place a story in such magazines.

"Tender is the Night" with its felicitous title, which recalls Keats and Scott Fitzgerald, is an even more belaboured attempt at such popular fiction. It seems also that in this story Duley makes use of her own earlier writings; hence the heroine's name, the house on Burst Heart Hill, the family shipping business and the employment of a choice between the men have their roots in the Brooking story mentioned earlier. It is even possible that this short story supplied the framework for what was possibly the novel *Octaves of Dawn* and did not grow out of her attempts to write such a novel. While the presence of a television set in "Tender is the Night" suggests that the story postdated the twenty working pages of the novel, it may possibly mean that it resulted from Duley's attempt to salvage something from the rejected manuscript.

In any event, a brief retelling of the plot of the story will reveal its vitality. Juliana Brooking, an upper-class girl, cannot decide whether to marry an American, Bob Courtney, who will take her to a colonial-style house in Virginia, or Ricky Calvert, a young Newfoundland doctor, who will take her to share the rigours of his practice in a northern outpost. While dancing at the Officers' Mess at Fort Pepperrell in St. John's, her intuition tells her to go home because something is wrong. Consequently, she learns that Ricky had had a motor-accident. Having bullied her way to Ricky's bedside, she whispers him back to consciousness with the promise she will wear parkas and snowshoes, if only she can walk with him. As they fall asleep with their heads on the same pillow, they feel secure in the belief that happiness can be achieved in a cold climate.

"Age Cannot Dither Her" is a much better story then the other two. It is interesting, therefore, that it is almost certainly Duley's last piece of writing. This is indicated by a notebook which shows not only the unsteady handwriting that commenced around 1956 but also contains jottings that connect it to the story; for example, the author writes about Lorna Collingwood, Christopher Scott and "The Big Dipper" bar at Gander, as well as snatches of dialogue. The notebook proves that Duley was working on a story three years after she returned from her European tour.

In the story Peter Scott of the United States Air Force is stranded at Gander International Airport waiting for a plane to fly him to a desk job in Goose Bay, Labrador. Jaded by the promiscuous sex in which he has indulged during the Korean War and disappointed on returning home to find that American women are too eager to be careerists ("to have" instead of "to be"), Scott is now looking for "a girl with the true feminine tincture." When an attractive woman walks into the airport, he is immediately fascinated by her. As if in response to the desires of Scott's fantasy concerning ideal feminity, Duley describes Lorna Collingwood's body in appropriately fantastic terms; "She looked super-physical, created in the grand manner like a Blake drawing for Paradise Lost and Regained." She is tall and slender and yet "large and Junoesque" as she moves "like vanguard action or like a magnificent stray from a leisured age when women sailed in billowing skirts." Similarly, this red haired, breathtaking woman is described as "a Titian model from Venetian galleries." Finally, as if to call attention to the pun in the title of her story on Shakespeare's line about

Cleopatra ("Age cannot wither her"), Duley describes Lorna as being "as central in a place as Cleopatra in her barge on the Nile." The reader is intrigued by this extravagant description of a young woman in a grey tailored suit and a touch of peachpink lipstick; and he becomes even more interested in her when a "fussy" man waves an admonishing finger at Lorna before he disappears behind an air-line desk.

Meanwhile, soon after the "fussy" man returns to reveal that she is a world-travelled child of fourteen who has been accustomed since the age of ten to being picked up and proposed to by strange men; in addition, Peter learns that such men are invariably shown her birth certificate by a Universal Aunt or Uncle or by a worried travel agent who has been asked to keep an eye on her. The author prepares the reader for Scott's eventual disillusion in this affair by emphasizing Lorna's "warmth, glow, soft contained gaiety, simplicity, [and] manners . . . [which contain] no suggestion of heat." One sympathizes nonetheless with his anger and chagrin at the revelation of her age: "He wanted to punish her, seduce her, put her in a glass case, send her a doll."

The vivid description of Gander Airport and the presentation of this regal child and her conversation are the distinguishing features of this story. It is disappointing, however, that the difficulties of creating a Zuleika Dobson-Lolita figure defeat the author and reduce her heroine to a budding sweetheart of Sigma Chi. Duley's language is simply not good enough for the wry comedy which seems to be the purpose of this surprise-package. The subject is as bold as that of *Novelty on Earth*; but Duley seems to have been somewhat uncertain of what effects might be achieved in such a story.

Duley's last book, *The Caribou Hut*, is an account of a wellknown hostel in St. John's during World War Two. As noted on the title page, the book "was sponsored by the St. John's War Services Association, and written in the early part of 1949, the year that Newfoundland gave up her independent status to become the tenth province of Canada." In 1948 the Executive of the War Services Association had wound up its affairs and gone into voluntary liquidation.[7] At that time the Association divided its surplus funds of about $8,000.00 between the Newfoundland Branch of the British Red Cross and the Great War Veterans' Association, but reserved approximately $800 for a history of the Caribou Hut which Duley was invited to write. There is no record that the resulting book was offered for sale, so that one assumes that most copies of it were presented to people who had been associated with the Hut. At any rate, the writing of the book appears to have been a labour of love, especially since the amount of money allocated by the War Services Association was probably barely enough to cover the expenses of printing. Consequently, the book, which seems to have been distributed only in Newfoundland, received no publicity and no reviews.

The Caribou Hut is in part a history of Newfoundland as well as a celebration of the civilians and fighters of the war years. As a result, the book is dedicated to Newfoundland: "To that loved land — and dearer still — the memory of the past" when "she lived her largest period of history [during which] . . . she was peacefully invaded" by the soldiers, sailors and airmen of the world. The book's black and white cover-design by Darroch MacGillivray is a fine drawing of "the Narrows," the entrance to St. John's harbour, and of the characteristic tall hills and box like houses on the north and south sides. The most important aspect of the book is the fact that it is very well written. While admitting that the climate of Newfoundland is "deranged," Duley nevertheless writes vivid and sympathetic descriptions of its landscape:

> There is a rich fullness and bleak emptiness — rock like geological skeletons. There is delayed spring, suddenly made delicate and beautiful the drifts of white pear-blossom flushed by the stalky Rhodora. Indigenous bloom comes from the shining Blue Flag, the Iris, that could so rightfully be called the fisherman's orchid. There is the purple blue smudge of the blueberries, whose low, speared leaves redden in autumn to stain the ground blood-red. On blueberry ground, autumn looks as if it had really murdered summer.[8]

The wind, which was always a torment to the author herself, is treated with affectionate tolerance and wit, as she describes its boisterous welcome to the native, who is comfortably

> sure he is back when he gets an orange-wrapper or a paper-bag full in the face. It is not unusual to pass a place where building is in progress, and receive a necklace of shavings, and on a big windy day, any Newfoundlander can read the news from the papers that blow around him.[9]

Duley is diverted from such preoccupations, however, by her shock at the arrangement by the British Government to give the Americans a ninety-nine year lease on territory in Newfoundland in exchange for fifty destroyers. As a result, she could not resist deriding the "Yanks" when they arrived in January 1940 in the huge transport, the *Edmund B. Alexander*. Wallopped by high seas, the ship "stayed uncomfortably off-shore fearful of the narrow entrance to St. John's. A salty townsfolk chuckled with mirth when the wonder-working Americans were brought in by a local skipper. Somehow that made things more equal when the vital young Americans overran the town." Even though the navigational code required a local skipper to bring the ship in, Duley had no inclination to be fair to grumblers who would not drink our water, who "became more vitamin-conscious wondering if the lack of summer-sun would take the enamel off their teeth," and who had enough luxuries to keep them happy in Siberia. Consequently, she gleefully states that the weather lived up to its reputation and the island, "like an unreconciled shrew . . . veiled her face in her finest fogs, making it difficult to see all the strangers." Similarly, the thunderstruck "livyers" shrewdly beached their boats and left off logging and minor construction to go to St. John's and Argentia to earn big pay for building bases on their bartered land. This account of the arrival of the Americans is perhaps a little malicious; but it does nevertheless reveal some facts about them as well as about the author. Writing about eight years after the fact, therefore, Duley still felt the need to chastise their arrogance, in spite of the fact that she had made friends with some of the American officers.

On the whole, however, *The Caribou Hut* is the sympathetically told story of how a small city coped with the thousands of servicemen who were getting out of hand because they had nowhere to go to spend their spare time. Special events, such as the visit of the young Frank Sinatra, were merely interludes which interrupted temporarily the favourite pastimes of brawling, breaking furniture in taverns, and throwing bottles. As a consequence, the St. John's War Services Association called a meeting to discuss this problem with the result that the plan for the servicemen's hostel was laid.

Duley's book gives the details of this plan by which billets in private homes were to be provided for men on leave, and a hospice would be established where the servicemen could eat, sleep, and be entertained. The name of "The Caribou Hut" was chosen for this hospice because "Caribou is the promise of rich, red meat for the isolated settlers" and because the animal had been the emblem of the Newfoundland Regiment since the 1914-1918 war. The Hut was opened on 23 December 1940 at the King George Fifth Institute on Water Street in St. John's.[10]

The arresting quality of her writing in this book is derived from Duley's accurate observations of the seething spirit of a garrison town that during the war years was swarming with uniforms, girls, and American dollars, as well as of the harbour that was often filled with ships which had arrived for repairs or to gain respite from submarine warfare. Some of these ships in St. John's harbour bore the marks of the terrible ordeal of the North Atlantic, as in the case of

> . . . the wreck that stood for so long with a great hole raised high above water-line through which the gulls swooped, to be lost to view for a second before they appeared on the other side.[11]

Such vivid recollections of wartime St. John's enliven greatly Duley's account of the Caribou Hut. Because she worked in the building herself along with many other volunteers, she had intimate knowledge of its operation by which she makes her little history vibrate with the thump of bowling balls, the splashes in the swimming pool, the pistol crack of endless rashers of bacon fried every day for five years and the ring of the cash register, as well as the sounds of music, dancing, and laughter. Similarly, she writes skilfull impressions of those ladies at the Hut who knew how to fry millions of eggs without getting bubbles in the whites, who sewed, darned, and pressed in the Home Room upstairs in order to keep the men looking smart when they went out socially, and who on baking-days had "hat and coat ready to run down the hill to the Caribou Hut" with homemade cakes that always had "icings in which the fingers could sink past the first-joint," and with sandwiches that were filled right to the edges of the bread. Such women may perhaps be forgiven for sometimes fussing about the colour of the kitchen smocks.

In a similar manner, Duley describes with considerable compassion the throngs of men that she observed in the Hut. They often seemed to her to be many pairs of hands that were outstretched to the cashier and servers who were often too busy to look up: and she describes those hands with chilling effect, for they are survivors' hands frost-bitten in icy water or scarred from burning oil or minus a finger, as well as young hands, gnarled hands, trembling hands; and they all belong to unsung heroes. Similarly, other servicemen are depicted by Duley as so many pairs of boots and feet that tell their own stories; there are, for example, the springy step of the young, untried fighter, the lurch of the drunk trying to blot out a frightful experience and the tap of a crutch, as well as "the muted step of a man creeping towards solitude." During her work at the hostel, Duley met all kinds of people and listened to all kinds of stories both funny and sad, as well as sarcastic and amiable; and many of them find a place in *The Caribou Hut*. As a result, she recalls in the book the laughing sailor who ate strawberries with pure joy and who underplayed the risks of convoy-duty. Similarly, we read about the torpedoed cat who had been to Dunkirk,[12] the airman who proposed by phone to his girl in Canada, the husband whose wife ran off with another man because she could not bear the buzz-bombs any longer, the clairvoyant young woman, the Lili Marlenes, the stories of rescued animals, the sea-bitten merchant-seamen who had reached saturation point, the romantic patriots, "the chucker-out" and the big-hearted Y.M.C.A. manager on guard outside the "sobering up" room; and they are all graphic witnesses to the realities of life in wartime St. John's.

The Caribou Hut is a lively, warm hearted and historically important book. As a result, the facts and statistics that it presents are greatly enlivened by Duley's discerning eye, crisp humour and compassion. In addition, the author's nostalgia over the demise of the old Newfoundland when it joined the Canadian Confederation is tempered by her hope for the future. As a result, she is willing to keep an open mind herself by giving Canada a chance: "like Churchill we do not view the future with any misgiving, but we know it is change, and we are experiencing the apprehension of the waiting-room." What Duley says of her homeland can be said with equal truth of her last book: "Whatever Newfoundland has been she was never trivial."

1. pp. 401-10.
2. · p. 407.
3. p. 402.
4. Written under the pseudonym of "N.F. Land," the story was rejected by *The Atlantic Monthly*; and the only known copy of it is the typescript in the Macmillan file.
5. (November 1943), pp 11, 50, 52, 55-56, 61-2, 65 and 85.
6. The typescripts of these stories with some pages of unidentifiable fiction were found among Duley's literary remains in a brown envelope post marked 1956 and bearing the heading *"The Family Herald*; Canada's only farm magazine." This may indicate that the stories were rejected for publication by this magazine, for they do not appear in its pages.

7. Minutes of meetings and other documents in Provincial Archives, Colonial Building, St. John's.
8. Margaret Duley, *The Caribou Hut* (Toronto, Ryerson Press, 1949), p. 4.
9. *Ibid.*, p. 8.
10. For a short account of how the building got its name and of Sir Wilfred Grenfell's association with it, see Paul O'Neill, *The Story of St. John's, Newfoundland*, Vol. 1, *The Oldest City* (Erin, Ontario, Press Porcepic, 1975), pp. 392-95.
11. *op. cit.*, p. 7.
12. See also 'Sea Dust' cited above.

CHAPTER NINE

The European Tour

Although it is difficult to follow her activities closely from 1942 to 1952, it is clear that Duley spent long periods away from home as she followed her familiar circuit of New York, North Carolina and Montreal during which she visited friends while usually staying at small residential hotels, and in each place revelled in the cultural attractions that were not available in St. John's. There is no evidence that she was writing at this time; and her income seems to have been modest; for it was probably limited to a few bonds, a little money from the estate, rent from intermittently letting the Rennies Mill Road house, royalties from her writing and an occasional windfall. It was a financially precarious way of life.

When she was in St. John's, she was busy doing war work, as she helped out at the Caribou Hut and worked with the St. John's Ambulance Corps. As stock-keeper at the headquarters of the Women's Patriotic Association, she sorted and packed thousands of home-knitted garments for the men overseas. From November 1947 to November 1950 she was a volunteer member of the Library Group of the Tuberculosis Sanitorium in St. John's and Corner Brook; and she later became the convenor of the organization. Finally, in 1951, she became vice-president of ZONTA, a club for professional women.

Duley's work with the library group enabled her to provide good books for the T.B. patients as she tactfully got rid of popular novels and magazines, by enticing many of the patients to read book-of-the-month selections, historical novels and biographies.[1] In addition, she lobbied the Library Group for money by stressing the fact that the improved reading habits of the patients made it necessary to buy up-to-date publications, especially as they "are reading book reviews and asking for the latest releases."

In December 1950 Duley gained "a paid job" when she became part-time Public Relations Officer with the Red Cross; and it was a post which, as she told Aunt Alice, "entails so much writing that long letters are impossible." Before this, from February 1949 to the fall of 1950, she seems to have been travelling;

but she probably came home before December because "Cyril has been very wretched for years — & this whole situation made me decide to stay after flying from Montreal with a return ticket in my pocket."

Her Report for 1951 as Public Relations Officer indicates that the "writing" she referred to in her letter to her aunt was hack work. Consequently, she wrote feature articles and news items for the local papers, as well as newsletters to be sent around the island. In addition, she helped to fulfill the request of Radio Station CJON that the Red Cross take over Ayre's "Greeting Time" as a service programme.[2] The plan of the programme was to interview out-of-town patients and to broadcast an account of their daily lives in the sanitorium to their families at home. Duley interviewed over two hundred persons and wrote many fifteen-hundred-word scripts that were put on the air daily from Monday through Friday from 25 October to 30 November. A couple of her notebooks of the time show that her Red Cross activities also enabled her to emphasize her feminist tendencies. Hence she wrote the broadcast talks on accomplished women such as Lucrezia Borgia, Florence Nightingale, and Jenny Lind, as well as Clara Barton, the American philantrophist, and Frances Willard, the American educator and reformer. All of this work Duley performed for $40 a month.

After Duley resigned the job with the Red Cross in 1952, she went to visit Gladys in North Carolina in April; but she was back in St. John's in May either because of Cyril's problems or because of her own difficulties with her tenant on Rennies Mill Road, "who only pays when she is brought into the Supreme Court." Litigation against this tenant was scheduled for June; but there is no record of such a lawsuit having taken place. As a result, the tenant remained in the house and Duley returned to the mainland.

But she was still very worried by Cyril's illness even as she hinted at an exciting plan for herself in a letter to Gladys: "I am quite ruthless in treading a certain pace, because I have a purpose, which if it doesn't come off at the present time, will only mean a date deferred. I can't admit to liking the set-up, and the tension is great, and life seeming circumscribed, as F's vigil is invariably from three in the afternoon to eleven at night." News of Cyril's deteriorating condition drew her home on 10 August; and he died a week later. She was deeply moved by his burial service: "It was a lovely day — the sun shone in the open grave — he was laid with Dad and Mother — the veterans dropped in poppies for remembrance — and the Masons evergreen for immortality."

Duley had reached a crossroads in her life. She was nearly fifty-eight years old, and her glamour as a novelist had faded: "I wonder what to do — but I have great faith in the pattern — have never been stuck in my life — and certainly don't expect to be now — It will all untangle as I untangle." The "purpose" that she had mentioned in her letter to Gladys in May was to visit England and Europe; and one suspects that she was thinking of living in England permanently and that difficulties with her tenant prevented her doing so. Having never crossed the English Channel, Duley was now determined to see France and Italy. As a result, she sailed from St. John's on the *Nova Scotia* on

30 October 1952, and arrived in Liverpool on 5 November.

The voyage did not lift from her mind the shadow cast by Cyril's death, so that she was dispirited and run down for a while as she indicated in a letter to Aunt Alice on 18 December from the Inverness Court Hotel in London: "It seems — I have seen them all off — & it almost looks as if Nfld. is a point of no return. It has all been incredibly sad — Daddy was the only one of them who died neatly and quickly." Sometime after Christmas in another letter to Aunt Alice, she outlined her plans for her European tour in March and promised to go to Somerset when she returned in April. While at the Inverness Court, she had been ill in bed twice; but she was averse to a doctor's advice concerning x-rays and "barium meals" because she felt that she was by no means "what the Christian Scientists call 'God's perfect child'." In spite of these difficulties, she was looking forward to seeing her father's family again. Because she had not been in England since 1935 when she had not visited her relatives, she only vaguely remembered Gwen and Freda Jefferies as "two infants sprawling between walking and crawling" from their visit to Newfoundland in 1913.

When her health improved, she spent January preparing scripts for four five-minute talks on the forthcoming coronation of Elizabeth II, which were to be broadcast on the well-known British Broadcasting Corporation programme "Calling from Britain to Newfoundland." This programe, which began during the Second World War, was directed by Margot Davies for nearly thirty years until it was ended by her death in 1972. Davies was the Newfoundland-born daughter of D. James Davies, an Englishman, who was a science teacher in St. John's, and who in 1934 became Newfoundland Trade Commissioner in London. Margot Davies' programme was inspired by her father's newsletter which was read on the B.B.C. Her own broadcast became popular in New-foundland immediately not only because it gave lonely servicemen an oppor-tunity to speak to friends and relatives at home but also because she worked hard at rounding up Newfoundlanders in England to speak on the air. Families in isolated communities, where letters were always late arriving, were over-joyed to hear their sons' voices telling them that they were all right. The programme had such a great effect on morale, in fact, that in 1944 Davies was invested with the order of M.B.E. at Buckingham Palace. In subequent years, the popularity of the programme continued to reflect the strong ties between Britain and Newfoundland so that after her death a plaque to her memory was placed in the lobby of Confederation Building in St. John's.

Duley's "coronation" talks, which went on the air in February and March 1952, were thus assured of a large audience in Newfoundland. In these broad-casts, she focussed on such aspects of the coronation as the bustle and the bunting in the streets, the regilding of the Golden Coach and the Coronation Chair which was "having its greatest spring-cleaning since Edward the First." In addition, she spoke of her amusement at some features of the event such as the amount of space assigned to guests in Westminister Abbey (peers and peeresses were allowed nineteen inches and commoners eighteen) and the various arrangements of silver balls and strawberry leaves that distinguished a duke's coronet from a baron's. In spite of the fact that these talks are pleasantly genuine, they are enlivened somewhat by Duley's admiration for the symbolism of the British Monarchy.

Similarly, in February Duley taped a talk to be broadcast in June which was called "The Town with the Flaming History," and which was later published in *The Listener* under an engraving from *The Illustrated London News* that depicted the great fire of 8 July 1892 in St. John's.[3] This script gives an impressionistic view of the city by describing its unusual harbour and moody climate, and by emphasizing the winds that had fanned other terrible fires during the nineteenth century.

Duley's European trip began on 17 March at Victoria Station, where she met her travelling companions and set out for Folkstone to catch the Channel boat. By writing to Gladys the next day, she started a series of letters that would grow into a kind of journal of her journey; hence in the first letter she describes the group of travellers as "fifteen strong from the good old USA-Canada-Bolivia and Britain — the whole making a motley gathering which has already jelled." The channel crossing was like a dream fulfilling itself as she kept repeating to herself "I'm in France." Soon she was travelling through the Somme country, and next through Arras to Amiens, where thoughts of the Royal Newfoundland Regiment and undoubtedly of her brother Lionel and Jack Clift came rushing to her mind: "I could only think of *them* and later when we arrived at Amiens — where I am now I went to the great wounded — dirty and devastated cathedral and found it full of pigeons in its roof — but so remindful of the 1914-18 war."

The Grand Hotel in Amiens, we are told, served a wonderful dinner and French wine is exquisite; but living in France is expensive and travelling through the country troublesome. The next morning Duley awoke in the Grand Hotel and ate her first continental breakfast which made her rave about the magic of French food in contrast with "the uninspired cooking of England." Within three hours of leaving Amiens, she arrived in Paris, which she already knew intimately in her imagination through her habit of arm-chair travel: "I knew it all — place de l'opera — jardin des Tuileries etc., — through long, nostalgic looking at a map."

Because Duley rarely dated her letters, it is difficult to be precise about her arrivals and departures. She apparently drove through Burgundy on 20 March and arrived in the early evening at Auxerre which she discovered to be a "quaint bunchy town — full of shattered houses — on narrow streets." As a result, she "made a bee-line for the cathedral where they were singing Benediction — so knelt for a while — & said French prayers."

Next day, the travellers were delayed on their journey to Geneva by an avalanche which blocked the roads. As a consequence, they were forced to take a detour that "wound around every precipice and gorge in Europe"; but the company amused themselves over the remaining fifty mountainous miles by singing and eating candy. When they finally arrived at the Hotel Richmond in Geneva, they were fortunate to be served a meal after the dining room had closed. "Scuppered," Duley fell into bed after rinsing out her nylons and bathing in "a stout, short bath like a doorstep." Like most North Americans, she was amused by the whimsicalities of European plumbing, as well as by the camaraderie of men and women who mingled in the washrooms "for the same common purpose."

The next morning, their courier gave the travellers a good tour of Geneva ("the cleanest town in Europe") and of the League of Nations; after which he waited for them to change their money before they set out along the Route Napoleon, which they were told was the road taken by Napoleon when he escaped from Elba and walked to Digne. The route took them "up a million miles it seemed. All snow-capped." Having passed through many mountains, the travellers reached the Ermitage Napoleon (a "modernized little gem" of a hotel) in the town in which the defeated emperor had stayed on his flight north. In this hotel also, Duley was amused by the facilities in her bathroom, but the description of such entertaining diversions in her letters soon gives way to astringent remarks about the affluence of post-war France:

> As comment I would say — that the way to win a war is to let your country go in tack to the enemy and then let other powers get it back for you. France seems to lack for nothing — all the hotels are central heated — the linen superb — and the food wonderful and piquant after austere England.

But she was aware that the French, like the British, had suffered during the war. As a result, her sympathies were aroused by a two-day drive through parts of the country where the underground resistance had been strong: ". . . and all along the way to Nice were monuments to little groups of the maquis who were shot on the spot — without trial — as the monuments to German brutality."

Duley was captivated by the city of Nice in spite of reminders of the barbarous treatment that had been given the *maquis* there; for her it was like "Florida in the the French tongue." That evening, the party went to Monte Carlo; and Duley's account of the Casino presents a marked contrast to her vivid descriptions of the beautiful gardens and orange trees lining the roads along the way. She depicts gambling rooms as dens of cynical pleasure-seekers; hence she scorns Monte Carlo as "the mythical principality which had the musical comedy touch — but there were no glamourous crooks — princes or diplomats — no beautiful mistresses in model gowns — no one but ordinary money grubbers — & grim faced croupiers bearing on their lips the last sneer in Europe."

Around 23 March, the travellers crossed the Italian border and drove along the Blue Coast of Italy with"thousands of carnations" and "signs of shell-spattered houses" in full view. Italy both enchanted and repelled her. Duley reached Santa Margherita Ligure by the long drive through Genoa, a city which she found "positively sinister," so that she had to keep reminding herself that "it was the cradle of Christopher Columbus & John Cabot and his son Sebastian." In addition, she was depressed by the "miles of decayed looking waterfront — tall dirty old stucco houses with swarms of people spawning in the streets" and by the "rows of washing hanging like banners from every window." Everywhere she looked she saw bugs as old as the houses. She was particularly disgusted by a filthy water-closet in a room which cost her too much money, so that she was glad to leave Genoa behind. But the beautiful Santa Magherita revived her spirits somewhat, for it was like "a set of gorgeous terraces, with palm trees, iris, calendula, pansies, all in gorgeous bloom."

Like France, Italy seemed to Duley to be quite prosperous: "if the spoils of war are the signs of victory *Italy* won the war." It grieved her that England had suffered so much; yet she was somehow exasperated that only in that country was austerity so obvious: "but truly, I believe they *love* discomfort. After all, their history did not start in 1914 — and even then they got no heat."

At Siena, the travellers concentrated on viewing architecture, painting, and sculpture, or as Duley wrote "on the works of art, exemplified by man at his highest development — instead of the works of God as illustrated in the cypress, the vineyards, the olive-trees, the camellia, orange trees — & the incredible clots of blossom." But nature was pushed from her mind for a time as she came under the spell of paint and stone; the black and white marble cathedral in Pisa seemed like a miracle to her, while she was enchanted by the mosaics and by familiar names associated with the city such as Cimabue. As a consequence, her thoughts went back "to that set of travel books I used to read on Sunday afternoons — the Stoddard set that Dad bought — & I know that the seeds of knowledge I had planted years ago were bearing fruit here & now. It seemed fair and right that I should be in Italy — because mentally I knew all about it."

After experiencing the wonders of Pisa and Siena, Duley was ecstatic over the three days that she spent in Rome, as she was overwhelmed by the splendour of the Sistine Chapel and the Vatican Museums. It seemed to her that these museums made all others look "like Woolworth's" and that 'Michael Angelo's ceiling' in the Sistine Chapel "was the greatest single effort in all time."

From Rome the travellers drove to Sorrento through country where Newfoundlanders had been stationed during the Second World War. In spite of a few holes left by wartime shelling, the countryside was rich with crops that were growing in drained marshes; and the fact that this was in Mussolini's Italy made her think of the American gangster Huey Long: just as "Huey Long, . . . had done much for Louisiana, so Mussolini had done much for internal Italy." After lunch in Sorrento, Duley and her fellow-travellers drove to Naples, which she discovered to be "the slum of Europe," particularly since it stank worse than Genoa. Pleased to leave Naples, she was overjoyed to visit Pompeii, which she had first read about in Fanny Badcock's room, and was enthralled to see that "the pictures of the ruins are exactly like the royal reader."

The next day the travellers sailed across the Mediterrean, which was "like blue grass," to the famous Blue Grotto on the island of Capri. At first sight, the Grotto appeared to be "nothing but a dark cavern in towering cliffs;" but when the sightseers were taken closer in an Italian rowing boat, Duley began to experience the remarkable effects of the place:

> The small boats enter the grotto by means of a chain, and as the low arch to the cave comes near the swarthy oarsman yells his one bit of English, 'lie down,' and instantly we flattened ourselves on the floor of the boat, almost scraping our scalps on the arch. Then inside the Grotto, the first moments are slightly tinged with fear & disappointment, but as the eyes readjust, the water all around becomes the most indescribable blue. Neither picture nor movies can recapture it — all I could find in my own words, is to say that the water is like a certain kind of blue glass, neither wholly blue; nor green or even aqua but definitely clear. It was an experience, like a fragment — a flash of beauty in all prevailing darkness.

As it was a calm day, the courier ordered the skipper of their boat to move around the island. As a result, they saw the famous villas in the area, including those of Gracie Fields and King Farouk. After this voyage, the travellers drove to San Michele, the mountain retreat of the Swedish doctor, Axel Munthe, who had built his home on the site of a Tiberian villa and who celebrated the joy of living there in *The Story of San Michele*. Duley was very impressed by Munthe's house, which lay on "unbelievable heights: "It is the only place I have met, where I wanted to set up my everlasting (earthly rest)." Duley thus resolved to read Munthe's book again.

Back in Sorrento, Duley wrote to Gladys about the wonderful day, while remarking that she had no interest in shopping madly with "the gang" between stops or in joining them in taking pictures: "I did not come to acquire — and brought little spending money — as I hold everything material now with very loose hands."

On the way back to Rome, the party was caught in a traffic jam that lasted for hours because of a motor race on the road between Naples and Rome: "There we sat for two hours watching the Italians maltreat their animals." Duley was greatly agitated by this delay and especially by the cruelty to animals that she saw: ". . . one of the agonies of travelling in Italy is the plight of the unloved animals. The cats are despised, the dogs muzzled, the borros lashed, while dragging the heaviest loads. And on a hill."

Having suffered through this ordeal, the travellers drove to the monastery at Cassino, the site of the famous hill-battle in 1944. Duley was so moved by this place that she reminded Gladys in her letter of the fact that the whole Christian world had been greatly shocked by the shelling of the Benedictine Abbey which had stood on its hill at Cassino since 509 A.D.: "Whatever one feels about it — it is considered the greatest act of ignorant vandalism of the war, but though the extenuators say the Germans were holding it as a look-out, no German body was ever found there. But I have no intention of condoning or blaming, I am merely reporting that we saw the whole spot, and lunched on the place that was called the 'Mad Mile' during the long shelling." Once again one senses ambivalence in Duley's attitude; on the one hand, she mourns the atrocities of war, but on the other, she seems somewhat bitter that Italy had been restored: "But in spite of prevailing destruction Cassino had been rebuilt under Marshall aid. Italy has been on the receiving end for so long that her wounds are almost mended. Unlike Britain which is still giving out. You would never recognize the present England from the one you knew — It is another world, & I can imagine now, why people travelling on the Continent are so discontented with Britain." As she reviewed the relative affluence of Italy and France, Duley was continually saddened by the postwar austerity of England as evidenced by the continuance of ration books and queues.

Having arrived back in Rome ill and exhausted, Duley, with the other travellers, set out the next day for Perugia, a place which held a particular fascination for her because of its nearness to Assisi. But before she could move around the place, she felt the need to refresh herself; her hair was so dirty she "did not care if Michael Angelo and Raphael were both in town — my first interest was a clean scalp." Having served her needs as best she could in the hotel, Duley concentrated on Assisi which she found to be enchanting.

St. Francis was her favourite saint because he was such a lover of animals and because he had "attained [to] such cosmic love that he could call the world his brother — (wish I could)!!" As Duley and her companions walked around the churches of Assisi, she heard a choir singing "the most pure Gregorian music with overtones for every Roman arch." The lay brother who showed them around looked to be about eighteen, although he was in fact thirty-five. The man seems to have affected her deeply because she sensed the freedom he had gained by accepting vows of chastity, obedience and poverty, and by thus "facing life with a rope around his waist." As a result, he exuded for her a strong sense of spiritual power and grace: "So much of Italy is religious without being spiritual that it was pleasant to meet true spirituality."

By the time Duley reached Florence, she was beginning to tire noticeably, so that she despaired of being able to write to Gladys about the city and its appeal for her. What she does write, however, shows her continued fascination with famous names of the past: "such names as Dante, Galileo, Michael Angelo and Giotto are as common as the Murphys in Nfld." This part of her letter-journal to Gladys indicates also that her interest in the illustrious past was just about saturated as she records that she found "too much grandeur" in the wonders of the Pitti Palace, and felt that the city walls were too confining. She and her companions, nevertheless, dutifully gaped at antiquities, were disrespectful about "the limbs of the mighty"; eventually, however, they all deserted culture and had a wild spree in the shops where they bought marvellous Florentine leather, straw-work and mosaic jewellery. After this, there is not a word in Duley's letter-journal about the splendours of the past to be found in European cities, in spite of the fact that she next visited Venice before returning to England by 18 April.

133

Shortly after her arrival in London, Duley visited her Aunt Alice Jefferies and family at Weston-Super-Mare in Somerset. She had looked forward not only to meeting these people but also because of her "deep approval of Freda's description of the non-human part of the family — I may say I love dogs — dote on cats." She did not feel so sure about the thousands of bees that Gwen kept, and wondered if they buzzed and stung in these large numbers: "Shall I arrive with a smoke screen?"

Even such minor fears were allayed, for the visit was an enormous success as she became part of a family again; and this new relationship with her aunt and her cousins developed and endured for the rest of her life. In the friendly atmosphere of the Jefferies home, the less artificial side of Duley's nature was nurtured as memories of her father were undoubtedly brought to her mind. Freda claimed that she did not rest until she had rediscovered the words and music of a hymn Mr. Duley used to sing: "It was a quest — and we saw countless people trying to find it. Eventually a fellow lecturer of mine, a staunch member of the Baptist Church, was able to produce it. It was a great joy to Margaret. The hymn was "'I am my Beloved's and He is Mine' as far as I remember." Freda was also aware that Duley "felt things very deeply and could be deeply hurt by unkind words . . . (although this did not occur while she was with us)."

Returning to London after this very pleasant interlude, Duley stayed at the De Vere Residential Club, while she kept pace with the increasing tempo of events as London prepared for the Coronation of Queen Elizabeth. She was delighted by the transformation of the city as the day approached; scaffolding, crash barriers and bunting seemed to be everywhere. She wrote to her Aunt Alice: "it seems as if every ancient monument is hidden by rows of water closets awaiting the human outpouring from far and near on the great day. The crowds are great — the jostling greater — and Hyde Park is full of tents." In spite of her fondness for the Monarchy, she nevertheless found some aspects of the occasion to be ludicrous. The thought of the gallons of urine to be expelled in London on the great day seemed preposterous to her as did the idea of putting the queen's face on a mug. Consequently, while buying one of these mugs as a momento for Gladys, she could not resist making the following remark about the commercial banality of the act: "How would you look on a mug? Even the undeniably good Royal puss finds it a bit of a strain."

About this time, Duley received the news from St. John's that her tenant had turned the Rennies Mill Road House into a shambles by putting in her own heating system. She later expressed her exasperation at this news in a letter to Gladys: "There is no furnace at 51 — Mrs. C . . . put in a beauty — paid around five cents — after which it was stripped out, leaving a hole and empty ends of pipes." In addition, the tenant had not paid any rent for seven months. Even though her lawyers were successful in pleading for an eviction, it is not known whether Duley was paid rent and damages. At any rate, she had to go home "to pick up the pieces," as she said to Aunt Alice, and "to make a new pattern and re-route myself": "It is just another upheaval — but experience has taught me

134

to be ready with passports etc. — & to be always vaccinated." Duley was obviously shaken by this episode, especially since she had not planned to return to Newfoundland at the time; but she reacted to it stoically enough: "as I have great faith in the pattern & the guiding hand — I do not mind being exploded periodically." This "pattern" was to become a recurring theme in her letters of the next nine years as she let down her defences and allowed her feelings to show to those, who, she felt, understood her best.

As a result, having booked air passage for 12 June, Duley continued to enjoy London, as she dined with friends, had supper at the Ivy with Flora Campbell, saw Shaw's *The Apple Cart*, and used a gift from Aunt Alice to go to a matinee of Wilde's *A Woman of No Importance*. In addition, she visited Stonehenge and Salisbury, and entertained Freda and Nora Jefferies, who came to London as her guests a week before the coronation. On 3 June she rehearsed at the B.B.C. for her talk "Town with the Flaming History" and delivered it on 4 June. She derived great pleasure from preparing and reading the broadcast, as she indicated in a letter to Gladys: "My script was not touched by the research department, the producer told me I was a 'treasure' endowed with a sense of timing and that my voice was like Lady Asquith's — 'very distinguished.' You can believe it or not — *but he said it* — and took me three times for tea and coffee — and as very interested male and female — How satisfactory it is — that interest is ageless." Duley was particularly pleased to be invited to give another talk any time that she returned to London. Meanwhile the Coronation Day of 2 June arrived, but the weather 'was [such] an abomination "that Duley watched the event on television: "I found the full Abbey service deeply moving — and much better than the pageantry outside." It is clear from this remark that she did not slip into Westminister Abbey as a gate crasher as was later claimed.

Before Duley left London for Newfoundland, she was pleased to be given a luncheon by her "Inverness Court friends — with whom I had daily contact for four and a half months. It was rather like going home and hearing all the news." Her final letters to Somerset before leaving England show clearly that she had come to love her father's family: ". . . as long as I inhabit this globe — I will write to you all — feeling it was good to have found you." Having left London on 12 June, she stopped for an hour in Iceland which struck her as the dreariest place she had ever seen ("like a top-secret bastion"). She was soon back in St. John's, however, and immediately began to "try and straighten out a seeming tangled skein."

It is interesting that during her stay in England Duley was reluctant to take even a small part in the literary scene when there was opportunity to do so. Her friend, Marguerite Lovat Dickson, had been back in England since 1944; and her husband, H. Lovat Dickson was an author and publisher, as well as a director of the London firm of Macmillan. As such, he was at the centre of the literary scene in London and could provide ready access to it for her. But Duley apparently remained deliberately aloof in this matter as Mrs. Lovat Dickson's recollections of those winter months in London in 1953 indicate:

> ... she stayed at a small family hotel in Bayswater. She made friends with the guests, and she appeared to be very happy writing, and seeing old friends. She was inclined to be secretive and kept her life in 'parcels' as well as her friends. When it was my turn to be 'opened' she would get in touch with me — we would meet — she would talk and talk — and sparkle; and then withdraw again. I never met any of her friends — and those of mine, like Gwen Graham,[4] the writer, she did not seem to care for. Even in London, when I gave a party for her, she appeared quite indifferent to meeting writers. I had imagined that living in Newfoundland and being cut off from that sort of society she would have enjoyed gossiping with other writers.

Duley herself confirmed this assessment of her behaviour in a letter to Aunt Alice that was written just before her return to Newfoundland: "I do not pour out my heart any more — perhaps — because in so doing — one *leaks* with emotions that weaken. I find it better to be a water-tight compartment." Such evidence seems to indicate that Duley deliberately detached herself from the literary scene; and, as such it implies her grave concern over her increasing inability to write. As a result, the experiences of her seven months abroad found expression only in her letter-journal to Gladys. At the age of fifty nine, therefore, she had written herself out; and she seemed to lack the ability and the inclination even to revise *Octaves of Dawn*.

1. Detailed information about Duley's work with the Association may be found in the files of the Red Cross.
2. Ayre and Sons is a Newfoundland firm with department stores and other business interests in St. John's and on the Mainland.
3. (11 June 1953), p. 962.
4. Gwethalyn Graham, author of *Earth and High Heaven* and *Swiss Sonata*.

CHAPTER TEN

The Remaining Years

Aunt Alice's letters to Duley when she was in England and after her return to Newfoundland were a comfort to her. As a result, Duley in her answering letters was not "a water-tight compartment" to that gentle woman as when she asked her, for example, to think of her "strongly" when she was in the air on 12 June and confessed she needed and cherished Mrs. Jefferies' thoughts: "for I am by no means as adequate inwardly as I appear on the outside. It has often been tough going — and sometimes so tempting to turn the face to the wall." In spite of this confession, however, only two and a half days after her arrival home, she was able to write Freda Jefferies that "such is the reclaiming power of one's native heath that I feel intensely local — partly, I suppose, because I stepped into the problems at once, and met many things foursquare." On 27 July, however, Duley did not seem to feel so "local" when in another letter to Freda Jefferies she remarked on the changes in St. John's since Confederation. The number of motor cars had increased alarmingly she reports, so that it was as easy to be run over at home as it was in Paris. In addition, since she herself seemed to be the only pedestrian in the city, Duley reflects upon the nature of the newfound prosperity in Newfoundland: ". . . they tell me most — or many — only have the first installment paid on them [the cars] — such is our flash Canadian prosperity." Even the plumbers and carpenters, she continues, whizz up "in big cars and dismount in plaid shirts." Not only could she herself not afford to buy a car but also she felt the disheartening prospect of paying for and supervising the conversion of her badly damaged house. Although Duley had some difficulty with the workmen, who frequently "took a spell" to have a smoke, the work of installing additional basins and toilets and refurnishing bedrooms was eventually completed so that parts of the house could be let out "as auxiliary hotel accommodation."

Throughout this episode, Duley, the pampered society girl, who had been used to maids since her birth, stoically and good-humouredly took up mop and broom and helped with the cleaning up. It was a harrowing experience for her at the time, but the "big job" did have its funny aspects that she promised to write about to Freda some day. As a result, Duley later used to regale her friends with imitations of the workmen's dialect and of her own assumed outrage at their blunt reports about screws and pipes such as "Missus, yer nipples is in wrong" or "Miss, the trouble is you needs to be lagged."

Duley thought the prospect of taking in roomers was interesting; so that, as if to slough off the skin of her old life, she said "good-bye to mahogany & gleaming walnut" and turned to bright colours and modern décor. With almost child-like glee, she wrote to Freda about the redecorating: "yesterday — I had a floor painted blood red — below ivory walls — which looks positively lurid — it is so damn cheerful." But the strain of the ordeal on her soon emerges in her letter as she reports that earlier in the week her confusion and exhaustion had prompted her to call in a Christian Science Healer and that "a talk with her restored my vision of eternal realities — so I can cope again. I literally could not exist without a measure of spiritual awareness — & I often look around — & wonder where people get their strength — ?" Consequently, Duley ends her letter to Freda on a note of hope as she quotes Christina Rossetti's words, "Does the road wind uphill all the way/Yes, to the very end . . . my friend," and refutes them by claiming that "there are little landings on all stairs where one can pause and rest awhile."

On 10 September, Duley wrote to her Aunt Alice that she was sitting at her desk in an ordered house with six rooms, two bathrooms, and a kitchenette in full use and that she preferred her present situation to any thought of the house as it had been or of the pattern of her own life at that time. As a consequence, she announces that that part of her life is over as she enters a new phase: "with the look of things my travelling days appear to be over — but there are many compensations. It is good to be in something I own — and to be able to move around in familiar space —" Duley was never to return to England or Europe; and, in addition, she visited Gladys in the United States only once in the remaining fifteen years of her life.

There is no doubt Duley was badly off financially at this time. Consequently, when the house was ready to bring in a modest income, she was willing to accept furniture and appointments as gifts and loans, especially since "the few isolated bits I owned looked lonely and ridiculous in large rooms." In a long letter to her Aunt Alice, Duley provides a detailed list of the gifts that she received at this time: "Florence lent me some good bits from Cyril's inheritance — as well as a couple of big oil paintings that Dad brought out from England — which settled back on the walls. After that a series of friends with excessive possessions began giving me presents." As a result, she accepted with grace many things, "some of which seemed magnificently generous," so that she felt like a bride being given a shower, "though no one came in with the groom." In addition, she writes to her aunt that she was "positively tearful with gratitude" for sheets, various linens, an electric toaster, iron, percolator, garbage can, plates, dishes, chairs, two blue velvet broad-loom carpets, two Liberty rug runners for the hall and an antique walnut chair. The common sense with which she accepted this help was as becoming to her as the generosity of her friends was to them. But the most exciting news in Duley's letter to her aunt is the report that she already has a young English mining engineer and a government official living in the house and is expecting the arrival of a young business woman at the end of the week.[1] Duley was pleased that she had achieved so much in the two months since her return to St. John's; and she was overjoyed shortly after when she received two cheques from the B.B.C. for a repeat recording of "The Town with the Flaming History" and for its publication in *The Listener*.

September 27 was Duley's fifty-ninth birthday; so that Florence and her nine-year-old daughter, Margot, took her to lunch at the Newfoundland Hotel. By now, she was tired of plaster, dust and workmen, as well as of looking after herself; and in addition, she had recently realized that she would have to let a fourth room in order to make ends meet; as a consequence, she was glad to relax on her "fiesta day." Thus she "lapped up a few gins" and found it to be "like a gift from high heaven to see the plate descending over my shoulder."

By 29 October, however, her spirits were higher than her fortunes, for the new venture had produced neither affluence, nor freedom from repairs, as she readily admitted in a letter to Aunt Alice. In the same letter, her display of ready wit indicates the extent to which she has learned to live with her new circumstances:

> Yet I thought that the Jinx had gone out of Rennies Mill. Subsequent events proved that it was only crouching on the door-step, waiting in the biblical manner, to return to the old haunts, now swept and garnished. I could not have worked hard enough in the mental realms to clean the upper air for a sequence of events started that seemed like the mad hatter's tea party — I had been out, and felt in a most harmonious mood, starting to get what the Catholics call a cold collation — I was opening a tin when it slipped and went straight to the bone of one of my fingers, and being a fainter I passed out feeling on the lip of death. Just at that moment a most important international company began ringing the doorbell to take a room — then a young guest's car burned in front of the door — my boiler burst magnificently while all I could do from the floor was to murmer 'every man for himself,' and bid the guests take to the boats.

That Duley enjoyed composing such well written letters at this time is well illustrated by the concise, piquant version of the above passage which she wrote in a letter to Gladys:

> By now I hope you have received my little air mail explaining the writing lapse. In retrospect that little gremlin period seems fantastic — I still have a feeling of myself lying on the floor with a foretaste of Abraham's bosom while all the bells were ringing, feet running, car burning, boiler

> bursting with me murmuring (more or less) nobly from the floor 'sauve
> qui peut' as the guests took to the boats . . . .

Such letters show not only the fact that Duley could still write as well as ever but also that she had an eye for comic detail which she never displayed in her novels.

Meanwhile the expenses of running her household were mounting because she had acquired "an excellent maid three times a week" and because she couldn't "be bothered with a bill now unless it was in three figures." In addition, the time of year brought painful memories of her brother Nelson to her mind, for October as the month for game in Newfoundland always reminded her of the large catch of partridge he always brought home, and especially so since he had been born in that month: "his birthday is on Hallowe'en and I never forget it as I find his passing the most poignant one in the family & so much like self-destruction —"

During the fall of 1953, Duley helped R. B. Job to prepare his memoir of his family for publication. Even when the book reached the galley stage, progress was slow because, as Duley claims, Job "seems in love with a new footnote every time we read. However the writer is a benevolent, rich man, and I am well looked after as we work." It is difficult to know how much of this memoir was written by Duley; but there is some evidence which suggests she may have composed most of it. In a letter to her Aunt Alice on 28 September 1953, she mentions that she was editing the book which she had "helped write three years ago"; and in another letter to Freda Jefferies, which was probably written in the early spring of 1954, she actually claims to have been the ghost-writer of the memoir. There is evidence also which suggests that R. B. Job paid her well for her services because he knew she was poor and because he respected her as a professional writer. The result of this collaboration between Duley and Job which was given the title of *John Job's Family Devon-Newfoundland-Liverpool 1730-1953*, was printed in 1953 by the St. John's Evening Telegram Printing Company and bound by Dicks and Company. The introductory foreword was written and signed by Duley and dated December 1949. Job not only expresses in the book his formal thanks to Duley for her help "in putting together the narrative" but also when the second edition was published he wrote the following inscription into her copy of the work: "The first copy goes to Maggie with my love and best thanks for her valuable assistance." But it is Duley's foreword which is of prime importance to this study, for it reveals much about Duley's own attitudes as she pays tribute to the Job family. As a consequence, her remarks are flattering to the author himself and to the "great many Jobs [who] have walked strongly across the Newfoundland scene"; and, in the process, Duley offers a vindication of the merchant princes who, according to the popular belief of the time, had persistently hindered the attempts to effect the union between Newfoundland and Canada. Duley's admiration for the Jobs seems genuine when one considers that both her letters and *The Caribou Hut* show a decided discontent with the proposition of Britain's oldest colony becoming the tenth province of Canada. In addition, her foreword to Job's book was written barely eight months after the coming of Confederation; with the result that her remarks are poignantly tinged with sadness at the thought of the old order changing and yielding place to the new:

Water Street is saturated with Newfoundland history. From its buildings, its coves leading down to the wharves, came the economy started by people like Samuel Bulley and the first John Job, the founders of the Newfoundland family. Over the old cobblepaved streets has rattled the island's provisions; and now curiously enough in 1949, since the advent of Confederation, old Water Street is paved and one hears a less dominant note, which seems to have settled down to become part of a greater whole.[2]

Duley's association with the writing of the Job memoir also provides some interesting insights into her personal life. It seems that she developed a romantic attachment to Bert Job and that he wanted to marry her. She was as secretive as ever about this relationship, so that her relatives in England did not even learn his name until January 1955; but it is worth noting that the affair did prompt her to reveal a little more than usual, as her letter to her Aunt Alice indicates. As a result, having revealed Bert's name to her, Duley writes about R. B. Job as the spitting image of General Smuts and claims that he had once been mistaken for Smuts in Hyde Park. In addition, she includes with the letter a photograph of the older Job in his garden at Topsail during the previous summer, as well as one of herself "lying dormant in a very large camera when I was taken in *December* picking a yellow rose," which was probably taken by R. B. Job just before the blizzard that occurred "between Xmas and New Year with twenty inches of snow."

Meanwhile, Christmas of 1953 was approaching when Duley wrote to Freda apologizing for the delay in answering her letter, and reiterating her steadfast principle that time and space did not interrupt relationships because the true meeting place of friends was in the heart. Duley's languuour, however, cannot be explained by the absence of her roomers on business: "With the lack of men on the landings I can stroll around in transparencies, so you can well imagine that adds to my present relaxation . . . there is no pleasure like paying-guests in the astral." By the same token, her lack of vitality cannot be accounted for by "the thrice-weekly appearance of an excellent maid," or by her declaration that she had been "trained in the grand manner to say 'we are in eternity now, so why hurry'." As she admitted, she knew "quite damn well" that she was spending an enormous amount of time lying down meditating. Her long morning and afternoon rests indicate that her strength was gradually lessening, although her social life seemed lively; for she told Freda that she had gone out to dinner "booted and spurred in my most glamourous gown well off the shoulders showing an infinite amount of skin."

While there are few extant letters from 1954, there are enough to give an accurate indication of Duley's activities at the time. In January Aunt Alice needed medical attention, so Duley sent Freda some kind advice about being prepared for any emergencies. On the whole, however, 1954 seems to have been a pleasant year in spite of "that lousy institution the kitchen sink." A friend visited her on the way to Liverpool via Boston and Newfoundland; and Duley provided a tea and a dinner while the ship was in port. Mr. Job was still attentive, and there was enough money for a few hats which she considered "so necessary to morale." She also bought a resplendent "new frock accordian pleated and seven yards round the tail." Meanwhile, Aunt Alice was holding her own and able to write to her niece again. Throughout such activities, Duley seems to have coasted along without much sense of direction; but she believed, nevertheless, that destiny would decide on a pattern of life for her. Although she wrote in a letter that the house was too expensive to maintain and that she was rapidly dissipating her capital, she did not seem agitated; and she added that her eye was "always on the increase of the loaves and fishes" and [that] there was a venturesome daffodil or two beginning to appear in the ice-cold spring.

Duley loved plays and went frequently to see the London Theatre Company, the English repertory group, which performed a different play each week from January until April in the 1950s. The performers often went to Duley's house on Rennies Mill Road for a night-cap after performances. In associating with these professional actors and actresses, Duley was in her element because she liked behaving dramatically and often "upstaged" her guests. At this time, then, she led as lively a social life as possible and continued to read a great deal. But the nightmare of Parkinson's disease was approaching.

Consequently, by 1955 Duley began to go down hill slowly as she indicated in a letter to Freda on 10 January: "I often feel like saying, 'How is your private hell to-day? Mine is burning me up.'" In spite of such feelings, however, she continued on the exhausting round of parties for Mary Quinn, who had flown home during Christmas; but Mrs. Quinn noticed a "steadiness and deliberation" in her movements. Some people thought that perhaps Duley had had a mild stroke. In any event, Florence Duley knew there was something wrong with her but decided not to broach the subject in view of her sister-in-law's silence. The mystery was solved some months later when the symptoms of Parkinson's Disease were diagnosed.

After the Christmas festivities were over, Duley was busy caring for her three roomers who were all ill with influenza; and she herself was feeling far from well at the time. But she put up as bold a front as possible, even to the extent of joking about her growing inclination to let her patients starve to death as their period of incapacity grew longer and longer. As a consequence of her own ill health, she wrote to Aunt Alice in March that she had been very frail all winter "due to a succession of missed heart-beats which cut off the oxygen from my brain leaving me in a world of grey clouds." Duley had resolved, therefore, to rest as much as possible and to keep her mind off herself by reading "chillers and thrillers instead of making my soul" and by trying to ignore her growing inability to care for the house. The viciously cold temperatures became a preoccupation with her at this time, so that she told Aunt Alice that New-foundland was a winter in her heart. In addition, she had lost "her hewer of wood and drawer of water" and was looking for a more efficient workman who would not "slosh grey water from a grey bucket." When she felt well enough, however, she continued to go to the weekly plays of the London Theatre Company.

By 2 June, when Duley wrote to Freda, the blizzards of winter had de-parted; but with an ill grace, for they left behind cold, damp, dripping days that seemed to draw "a positive all round De Profundis from a creaking popula-tion." It is clear that the weather depressed Duley and, in addition, as she wrote to Freda, it was hurting the crops and creating "the most purgatorial scene that Dante could imagine." Consequently, she yearned "for kinder skies and softer air than Nfld. will ever concede. Like all wild witchlike places the country can be magnificent — but who wants to live in magnificence that is too heavy for human flesh & bones." It seems that at this time Duley could find only futility and despair in everything. A week earlier, for instance, an impressive group of four thousand, singing Portuguese fishermen had paraded through the streets of St. John's to carry a statue of "Our Lady of Fatima" as a good-will offering to the Roman Catholic Basilica, the church at which many such seamen had worshipped over the years, as well as to the city itself, which had been a haven for the Portuguese "white" fleet for centuries. But Duley was so unimpressed with this spectacle that she calls it "grotesque" in a letter to Freda and condemns the chanting of the fishermen as if it "came from ghosts within white sea fog writhing through foggy streets." Duley's discontent with unfavourable weather clearly affected her judgment in this matter, just as she saw something humor-ously grotesque in another incident that she relates in the same letter. As a result, she tells Freda about the plan of the Civil Defence organization to drop mock-bombs on St. John's so that the people of the city could be shown how it might be evacuated in case of an aerial attack. When the appointed time of the exercise arrived, however, not a single plane left the ground because of the thick fog; and Duley's wry deduction concerning this failure is the claim that the best defence against an attack on Newfoundland is its weather and not anti-aircraft guns. Such remarks in her letters indicate how very grim and foreboding the spring of 1955 was for Duley; in fact, the only bright spot in it seems to have been the great pleasure she took in caring for four stray Persian kittens and seven finches from Montreal which had escaped from an exhibi-tion.

By July the improved weather raised Duley's spirits a little; and she bought some new clothes to raise them even higher and gave some consideration to Glady's constant invitation to visit her. She realized all along, however, that she could not afford such a trip: ". . . it would be infinitely more expensive than going to Europe — & at present I couldn't afford a slice of bread or a caraway seed." By September, her concern for Aunt Alice and the thought of the renewed burden that her relapse had placed on Freda caused her to forget her own ills to some extent. Her aunt's death before the end of the month was nevertheless a great shock to her, so that she wrote immediately to Freda to comfort her and to caution her not "to raise the barrier of grief" and thereby to block the "surge of love" which is "the true communion."

Duley visited Gladys in the States the following Christmas and stayed on for January and part of February because she needed respite "from the rigours of the N. Atlantic." Meanwhile, her illness had worsened to the extent that people began to observe physical incapacity in her. Mrs. C. Blackwell of Winston-Salem, for instance, recalled that during a game of cards Duley "would 'inch' her cards across the table so that the tremble would not be obvious." But it was not until 6 January 1959 in a letter to Freda that Duley finally admitted that she had an "indisputable illness." Meanwhile, one can trace the debilitating effects of her illness as well as her bravery in the face of it, in the couple of letters to Freda that were written in the intervening years.

In a badly-typed letter of 4 February 1957, which ends with a wobbly handwritten postscript, Duley reveals the great difficulties she was encountering in running the house on Rennies Mill Road. Putting up a bold front by joking about these calamities, she makes it clear that she was hard pressed by them as when the furnace failed and the pipes burst so that the place became a kind of skating rink ("and of course I couldn't find my skates"). Similarly, while enduring the cold as repairs were made, she jokes about her teeth "rattling like castenets." In addition, a troublesome skin disease caused her nylon stockings to rip continually ("since I stopped ringing the bell I snag and snag"). Because Freda had written about some ailment of her own, Duley responds with a more serious assessment of her own physical frailty: "What a plague the body is. I have to force myself to keep going or I would turn my face to the wall — but I am always deeply aware of other forms of power that can rush in if the right contacts are made." Perhaps because of such preoccupations, she is moved to express sadness over the illness of Anthony Eden: "I think he is important historically and did what badly needed doing — which action, at least woke up the world, and certainly the U.S. who are still hopping mad with Eden." In addition to her own physical problems, however, the upkeep of the house was draining her money so that she told Freda she was considering selling it in the spring.

Meanwhile, Duley forced herself to leave the house whenever she could, sometimes merely to collect money for the S.P.C.A. She seems to have been revived somewhat at this time, probably because of her readings, as she hinted in her letter to Freda on 11 January 1958: "I have taken up science and read it all the time. Having read so much Metaphysics I find the outer search for The Unified Field the same as the search for God — it has become an enthusiasm with me and I am lost in atoms." By 1959, however, her right hand had become crippled, so that she was reduced to "bribing" young Margot to write her letters for her. While others also helped her in this way, she continued to try her own hand at typing her letters as she did to Freda on Twelfth Night 1959. In this letter, Duley readily admits how fortunate she had been to be able to go to Florence's for Christmas Day; but she masks her incapacity somewhat by referring humourously to her predicaments: "Transported bodily in the most handsome crimson velvet dressing-gown in which I looked like one of Pope John's new cardinals." For some time after this, Florence cooked her a hot meal nearly every day which young Margot brought to her after school; and others also brought her food from time to time.

It seems that Duley could never bring herself to name the disease which was killing her; instead, as she reported to Freda, she would say only that her doctors had given her condition a fancy name which she would not repeat "for fear of giving it greater reality believing as I do that symptoms are only relative." She was later more precise about her illness and its treatment in a letter to Freda in January 1959 in which she speaks of having had "a severe reaction from modern drugs which made me feel as if the end was in sight until they finally found something for ten days retching . . . I finally could swallow an egg-[nog] laced with [whiskey] which I am sure I got down for the [sake] of the spirits." This badly-typed letter is perhaps the last she attempted to compose and type by herself; it is interesting, therefore, to note its almost wistful, nostalgic tone as she recalls Gwen's bees in the garden at Weston-super-Mare:

> Last summer a bee came in as big as a mouse and literally crawled round on the floor and I [kept] [thinking] of Gwen and her hives full of nasty buzz — I can't think of [getting] out until the snow goes — everything must come to me even the [hairdresser] — I wouldn't mind a few of those wind-[blown] jaunts protrayed in the family snaps but for this slice of life, I imagine [my] travelling days are gone.

Such imaginative recollections of better times contrast vividly with the suggested neurosurgery which Duley, according to some of her friends, refused even to consider at this time.

Although she was still at 51 Rennies Mill Road in July 1959, and Margot was by now writing her letters for her, Duley was less and less able to look after herself. A neighbour found her one day at the kitchen table eating peaches out of a tin. As a consequence, sometime between July 1959 and January 1960, Florence took her to live with her in the house on Monkstown Road that Great Aunt Chancey had left to Cyril. Here she stayed for nearly seven years, tended as an invalid by Florence and Margot and watching with pleasure the development of her niece's personality and intellect.

Duley continued to dictate letters to Somerset but with time they became more and more nostalgic, quiet in tone and resigned in attitude. One can see in these letters also the author's imagination at work as the blossoming pear tree in Bath for example, becomes in her memory a flowering cherry. In reality, however, Duley knew that her own house just around the corner could get on without her; indeed, she said she could easily let everything slip out of her hands even though she had to put on a new roof. But the handling of such tasks fell more and more to Florence's lot. In addition to her job, therefore, she took on the responsibility of Duley's rents and tenants, as well as spending with her as much time as she could when she was at home. In the daytime meanwhile, Duley was sometimes lonely, and in a letter dictated to Freda on 4 August 1961 she confesses that she yearned "to ring the bell." But the old days, when there were maids to answer every push of the finger, were no more. By this time, Duley saw only the closest of friends; and some had been asked not to come again because she could not bear for them to see her at her worst. In spite of the fact that her eyes were failing, she bought a T.V. set; but she sold it the next week because "the commercials were driving [her] nuts." And all the while, as she commented dispassionately, she was amazed that her body would take such a beating.

Under these circumstances, the many telephone calls to and from Gladys helped Duley, as she reiterated in a letter to Gladys the joy that these conversations brought to her: "I leave the phone full of espirit d'escalier'. . . Sometimes I wonder if I'll make it without going whacky! One of my shoulders will not shake in harmony with the other and I often wake up beating my breast." Duley and Gladys had always been close, so that she was overjoyed when Gladys came home to visit her in July 1962; but after the visit Duley "was more lonely than ever."

Duley's remaining years wore slowly away; but she continued to take an intellectual interest in the world around her. Although she was impressed by technological advances, it seems that she felt that things might be moving too fast for the moral good of society as she wrote to Freda in 1962: "We are living in a most remarkable age most of which we do not understand. However it seems to me as if everything and everybody is on the march. I find the brutality in all the papers very sick making so I have given up reading them." In Duley's last letter to Freda, which was dictated in 1965 or 1966, she thanks her for the gift of a light, fleecy scarf to drape over her nightgowns, and tells her that she has not been fully dressed for four years. No signs of resentment appear in these letters but Duley does express annoyance when a substitute is sent for her favorite V.O.N. nurse.

The saddest thing about Duley's last years is the fact that her bright mind became dim, so that she would sometimes dress herself as elegantly as ever and walk to Murphy's Grocery on Rawlin's Cross, only to be led gently back home by one of the staff. By this time, her friends stopped visiting her because she recognized them for a fleeting moment only; there was no point of contact left. When Florence could no longer cope, Duley was placed in St. Luke's Homes in St. John's where she died on 22 March 1968 after a year of hallucination and mindless oblivion.

Three days later on 25 March, Muriel Rogerson wrote Freda Jefferies about her death:

> It is a sad thing to do telling of dear Margaret's passing on Friday after eight long years of illness & the last four not knowing much of the outside world. This afternoon she was laid to rest. The service was held in

the Memorial Chapel of the Funeral Home. A simple lovely service & about fifty old friends attended. As we were singing the hymn a shaft of sunshine glowed through the chapel. Flowers only from Gladys and family. Florence as usual did everything. What a wonderful sister-in-law she has been. The last ten days Margaret was in a coma & just slept away. She was very thin, but didn't suffer any pain which one can be thankful for.

Duley's will names Florence as her beneficiary; and it is important to note that this document was written in 1957 and therefore long before she moved to Monkstown Road to be cared for by Florence and Margot. As such, the will is a remarkable tribute to the love and concern that Duley enjoyed over the last years.

An equally fine tribute to Duley herself is the fact that Freda Jefferies kept the Somerset letters and thereby retained a valuable diary of the last fifteen years of the author's life. These letters, some of which are to her Aunt Alice but most of which are to Freda, attest not only to the strong bonds of friendship and concern among the three women but also to the fine qualities of Duley's mind and writings. It is fitting that the final word in this book should be Margaret Duley's as she writes these letters which are full of gaiety, weariness, humour, patience, advice, bravery masquerading as vanity, delightful references to cats and dogs, graphic descriptions of the weather, particularly of winter's whims, vignettes of St. John's in the early years of Confederation, shrewd comments on current affairs, religious reflections, warm messages to the family to buy sherry with her money order so that they may all toast one another in spirit across the Ocean at Christmas, and reports about her beloved niece. As a result, we read of Margot spurning the Brownies because they do nothing but sing "Farmer in the Dell;" Margot as scribe, waiting to get away to play baseball; and of Margot at fourteen determined to be a doctor and using her bedroom as an observation base for "a kitten in embalming fluid," while her aunt prays "its soul out of Purgatory." Yet in all this there is scarcely a word about writing. When Freda showed interest in *Highway to Valour*, Duley told her she would send her a copy and added that she had written it "on the backs of envelopes while coping with a web that grew bigger and bigger." Duley is thus enigmatic to the end about her own writing; although, one must add, that to her credit she never once spoke of being neglected as a writer at home. But she did hint to Cutty Kitchell that she had thought about the response of her countrymen to her writings; and it is fitting, I think, that her remark on this matter should end this discussion of Duley's life and work: "I have left them a heritage. In their library will be a little corner of Margaret Duley's works."

---

1. The person was Citty Galen; later Mrs. C. B. Ketcheg.
2. Foreword, p. 14.

BIBLIOGRAPHY

1. Unpublished Sources

B.B.C. File: Margart Duley's correspondence with Robert Goodyear of the Talks Department of the British Broadcasting Company about her broadcast "Town with the Flaming History" on 4 June 1953; the text of the talk was published in the *Listener*, and the four "coronation talks" given on the overseas programme, "Calling from Britain to Newfoundland."

Duley MS: four MS note-books; the typescripts of four, presumably unpublished, short stories; twenty typed pages of a novel, possible *Octaves of Dawn*; a set of proof sheets of "Mother Boggan;" a copy of Mrs. Duley's unprobated will, numerous family photographs, family letters, notes from Gladys Duley Courtney; and the remains of Margaret's library.

European Journal: a report written almost daily by Margaret Duley to her sister Gladys chronicling her journey through France and Italy in March and April 1953.

Macmillan File: correspondence with the Macmillan Company of Canada about the publication of *Highway to Valour* and *Novelty on Earth;* readers' impressions, publicity material, reviews, a script of a short story, "Granny goes the Last Mile," together with an unidentified coloured sketch of a Newfoundland scene; letters from Marguerite Lovat Dickson, who read for Macmillans, to Ellen Elliott, a director of the firm; letters to and from Margaret Duley and Ellen Elliott which combine personal and business matters to such an extent that the author said if it was not etiquette "your secretary can perhaps take the scissors and put bits and pieces on the file."

Miscellany: letters and recollections from Margaret Duley's friends and acquaintances; taped interviews; Margaret Duley's scrapbook with reviews, photographs, dust-covers, etc.

Red Cross File: copies of the reports by Margaret Duley for the period when she was Public Relations Officer for the local branch of the Canadian Red Cross.

The Somerset Letters: about forty letters to Margaret Duley's first cousin and aunt, Freda Jefferies, and Mrs. Edward Jefferies respectively, in Weston-Super-Mare, Somerset, England. These letters written between 1952 and 1962 are in Margaret's hand until 1959(?) when Parkinson's Disease made dictation necessary. There is one letter from Freda Jefferies; and the one from Muriel Rogerson announces Margaret's death and describes her funeral in March 1968.

2. Published Sources

Books by Margaret Duley

The Eyes of the Gull (London, Arthur Barker Limited, 1936).
Cold Pastoral (London, Hutchinson and Company, 1939).
Highway to Valour (Toronto, The Macmillan Company of Canada; 1941).
Highway to Valour (The Macmillan Company, New York, 1941).
Highway to Valour (London, Methuen & Co., Ltd. 1943).
Novelty on Earth (New York, The Macmillan Company, 1942).
Novelty on Earth (Toronto, The Macmillan Company of Canada, 1942).
Green Afternoon (London, Methuen & Co., Ltd., 1944). English edition of *Novelty on Earth*.
Så Stred Sara (Stockholm, Sohlmans, 1946). Swedish edition (*How Sara Struggled*) of *Novelty on Earth*, translated from the English by Tore Zetterholm and Nils H. Gyllenbaga.
The Caribou Hut (Toronto, the Ryerson Press, 1949).

Reprints:

The Eyes of the Gull (Toronto, Griffin House, 1976).
Cold Pastoral (Toronto, Griffin House, 1977).
Highway to Valour (Toronto, Griffin House, 1977).

Other Writings by Margaret Duley

"Cold Pastoral," an excerpt in *From This Place*: a selection of writings by women of Newfoundland and Labrador, ed. Bernice Morgan, Helen Porter and Geraldine Rubia (St. John's, Jesperson Press, 1977), pp 26-33.
"The Healer," an excerpt from *Highway to Valour* in *By Great Waters*: a New-foundland and Labrador Anthology, ed. Patrick O'Flaherty and Peter Neary (University of Toronto Press, 1974), pp. 198-209.
"Sea Dust," *Chatelaine* (November 1943), pp. 10-11; 50-2; 55-6; 62; 63; 65; 85.
"Mother Boggan," *Fortnightly* (April 1940), pp. 401-10.
Foreword (December 1949) Job, Robert Brown, *John Job's Family, Devon-Newfoundland-Liverpool 1730 to 1953*: A story of his ancestors and successors and their business connections with Newfoundland and Liverpool 1730-1953 (St. John's, Newfoundland, The Telegram Printing Company Limited, 1953). Second edition 1954.
"Glimpses into Newfoundland Literature," *Atlantic Guardian* (July 1956), pp. 20-27.
Verses in *A Pair of Grey Socks*, A First World War Story by Mrs. T. J. Duley, n.d., no publisher named. Probably written between 1914 and 1918.

Essays about Margaret Duley

Feder, Alison, "Margaret Duley: Still Unknown Novelist?" *A Room Of One's Own,* Vol. 5, No. 3, 1980, pp. 60-69.

Morrow, Margot Duley, "Margaret Duley 1894-1968," biographical introduction for the reprints by Griffin House of *The Eyes of the Gull, Cold Pastoral* and *Highway to Valour.* Bound only with *Highway to Valour.*

O'Flaherty, Patrick, "Margaret Duley and Newfoundland," *Dalhousie Review* (Winter 1977-1978), pp. 634-44.

——, "A New Look at Margaret Duley," *Journal of Canadian Fiction,* No. 21 (1977-1978), pp. 124-26.

——, "Margaret Duley's fiction 1936-42" in *The Rock Observed: Studies in Newfoundland Literature,* University of Toronto Press 1979), pp. 127-143.

Rhodenizer, Vernon Blair, Canadian Literature in English (Montreal Quality Press, 1965), p. 760.

Story, George M., "Margaret Duley: 1894-1968," *Newfoundland Quarterly* (Winter 1975), pp. 15-16. Text of an address given to the Writers' Guild on the occasion of the Margaret Duley Fiction Awards, St. John's, 13 December 1974. Reprinted in *The Blasty Bouch,* ed. Clyde Rose (Breakwater Books, 1976), pp. 193-96.

Story, Nora, *Oxford Companion to Canadian History and Literature* (Oxford University Press, Canadian branch, 1967), p. 231.

Whalen, Linda, "Margaret Duley: a critical analysis," *Newfoundland Quarterly* (Winter 1975), pp. 27-29.

Whiteway, Dr. Louise, "*History of the Arts in Newfoundland,*" *Newfoundland Government Bulletin* (January-March 1953), pp. 3-16. Only small reference to Miss Duley.

"Success of Local Novelist," *The Daily News,* St. John's, Newfoundland (30 April 1941), p. 4.

Notices and Reviews

The Eyes of the Gull:

"The Eyes of the Gull," *The Evening Telegram,* St. John's, Newfoundland (19 November 1936), p. 17. R. P. Duder.

"The Eyes of the Gull," *Sunday Mercury,* Birmingham, England (8 November 1936), p. 8.

"The Eyes of the Gull," *The Reading Evening Gazette,* (9 November 1936), p. 4.

"Love on an Island," *Observer,* London, England (15 November 1936), p. 188. G. W.

"The Eyes of the Gull," *Manchester Guardian* (23 October 1936), p. 7. Charles Marriott.

"The Eyes of the Gull," *The Yorkshire Herald* (19 November 1936), p. 3. S.M.T.

"Helluland Romance," *Overseas Daily Mail* (24 October 1936), p. 16.

"Some Novels of the Week," *Public Opinion* (6 November 1936), p. 462.

"Newfoundland Tragedy," *Times Literary Supplement* (28 November 1936), p. 993.

"The Eyes of the Gull," *The Gazette*, Memorial University of Newfoundland (4 February 1977), p. 5. Alison Feder.

"Province's First Novelist Gets Attention Again," *The Evening Telegram*, St. John's, Newfoundland (16 April 1977), p. 14. Helen Porter.

"The Eyes of the Gull," *Newfoundland Quarterly* (Winter 1977), p. 14. Linda Whalen.

"The Eyes of the Gull," *Canadian Book Review Annual, 1976*, ed. Dean and Nancy Tudor and Linda Biesenthal (Toronto, Peter Martin Associates, 1977), pp. 127-28. Patricia Galloway.

"The Eyes of the Gull," *Newfoundland Herald TV Week* (9 February - 15 February 1980), p. 104. Gervase Gallant.

Cold Pastoral:

"A Newfoundland Novel," *The Daily News*, St. John's, Newfoundland (4 November 1939), p. 5. H.B., i.e. Grace Butt.

"Cold Pastoral," *The Gazette*, Memorial University of Newfoundland (June 1977), p. 12. Alison Feder.

"Province's First Novel Gets Attention Again," *Evening Telegram*, St. John's, Newfoundland (16 April 1977), p. 14. Helen Porter.

Highway to Valour:

"Woman Novelist is Influenced by Newfoundland's Bleakness," *The Free Press*, London, Ontario (4 October 1941), p. 32.

"Highway to Valour," *Christian Century* (October 1941), p. 1213.

"Highway to Valour," *Wisconsin Library Bulletin* (December 1941), p. 201.

"What's New in Print?" *Curtain Call* (December 1941), p. 10. R. H. W.

"Magic of Wild Newfoundland Gives Novel Sibelius Touch," *Toronto Daily Star* (27 September 1941), p. 10 M. H.

"Tragedy and Disaster," *Winnipeg Evening Tribune* (11 October 1941), p. 21. M. R.

"Novels of Unusual Merit," *Saturday Night* (27 September 1941), p. 24. A. F. Gerald.

"In Newfoundland," *The New York Times Book Review* (28 September 1941), p. 26. Jane Spence Southron. Reprinted in *The Daily News*, St. John's, Newfoundland (4 October 1941), p. 7.

"Highway to Valour," *The Narrator: Devoted to Books* (October 1941), p. 19. Pearl McCarthy. Official Publication for the Literary Guild in Canada.

"Highway to Valour," *The Windsor Star* (4 October 1941), p. 2. J. J. Dingman.

"Sea, Love and Death," *The Globe and Mail* (4 October 1941), p. 8.

"Highway to Valour," *New York Herald Tribune* (28 September 1941), p. 10.

"A Heroine Meets Three Tragedies," *Kansas City Star* (20 September 1941), p. 14-D.

"Novel of the Week," *Ottawa Journal* (27 September 1941), p. 21.

"Highway to Valour," *Library Journal* (August 1941), p. 669.

"Curtain is Lifted Upon Love in Newfoundland," *The Montreal Star* (20 September 1941), p. 24. H.O.H., i.e. Harvey O. Higgins.

"Highway to Valour," *Cleveland Open Shelf* (October 1941), p. 20.

"Highway to Valour," *Saturday Review of Literature* (11 October 1941), p. 13. R. L. Nathan.

"Highway to Valour," *Booklist* (15 November 1941), p. 95.

"Highway to Valour," *Buffalo Evening News* (27 September 1941), p. 7. M.L.S.

"Highway to Valour," *Farmer's Magazine* (November 1941), p. 53.

"In Newfoundland," *Hamilton Spectator* (20 December 1941), p. 9.

"English-Canadian Letters," *University of Toronto Quarterly* (April 1942), p. 304. J. R. MacGillivray.

". . . Strange Tale with a Touch of Mysticism," *The Daily News*, St. John's (23 September 1941), E. Y. p. 4.

"Fiction in Brief: Speed and Colour," *Times Literary Supplement* (3 April 1943), p. 165.

"Highway to Valour," *Manchester Guardian* (2 April 1943), p. 2.

"New Novels," *The Observer* (28 March 1953), p. 3. Alan Pryce-Jones.

"Highway to Valour," *Calgary Herald* (25 October 1941), p. 12.

"That Grey and Lonely [sic] Land," *The Daily News*, St. John's, Newfoundland (16 April 1953), p. 5. L.C.M.

"Highway to Valour," *Newfoundland Quarterly*, Special Issue (Spring 1978), p. 32. Alison Feder.

"Highway to Valour," *Quill and Quire* (December 1977), p. 30. Linda Whalen.

"The Elements of Newfoundland," *The Atlantic Provinces Book Review*, n.d. Presumably 1978, p. 3. Gwendolyn Davies.

"An Author and a People Rooted in Rock," *Ottawa Journal* (4 February 1978), p. 46.

Novelty on Earth:

"Novelty on Earth," *Booklist* (15 June 1942), p. 384.

"Drama of Great Romance Between two Mature People," *The Montreal Star* (13 June 1942), p. 22. S. Morgan-Powell.

"Problems of a Widow's Love," *The Globe and Mail* (16 May 1942), p. 10.

"Novelty on Earth," *Books* (10 May 1942), p. 2

"Miss Duley Offers New Stirring Novel," *Winston-Salem Journal* (17 May 1942), p. 530. J. R. Newby.

"Wit From Newfoundland," *Saturday Night* (30 May 1942), p. 17.

"Good Love Story," *Winnipeg Free Press* (30 May 1942), p. 13. A. C.

"Sophisticated Study of Women," *The Free Press, London, Ontario* (6 June 1942), *p. 29.*

"*Novelty on Earth*" in "*Saturday Sun Magazine*" *Vancouver Sun*, (30 May 1942), p. 4.

"Novelty on Earth," *The Narrator: Devoted to Books* (May 1942), p. 4.

"The Laughter of Adult Minds," *New York Herald Tribune Books*, (10 May 1942), p. 2. Rose Feld.

"A Dramatic Story," *The New York Times Book Review* (10 May 1942), p. 7. Jane Spence Southron.

"Age-Old Theme Makes Good Novel," *Greensboro Daily News*, (10 May 1942), p. 2. A. N.

"A Satiric Twist to Triangle Plot," *The Montreal Gazette* (23 May 1942), p. 9. Eleanor Wood.

"Conversational Love Story," *Springfield Union and Republican* (24 May 1942), p. 297. L. S. Munn.

"Four Novels: Light Entertainment," *Kingston Whig Standard* (9 June 1942), p. 4. Samuel Marchbanks.

"Other New Novels," *The Ottawa Journal* (30 May 1942), p. 23.

"Modern Romance," *Hamilton Spectator* (30 May 1942), p. 9. J. I. M.

"And Three's a Crowd," *Windsor Daily Star* (16 May 1942), p. 3.

"Unusual Triangle," *The Toronto Daily Star* (16 May 1942), p. 10. M. H.

"Green Afternoon" in Jane Marshall's "Time Off For a Book," *Good Housekeeping*, British edition (April 1944), p. 46.

"Green Afternoon," *Manchester Guardian* (11 February 1944), p. 3.

"New Novels," *The Observer* (6 February 1944).

"Green Afternoon," Birmingham, *Sunday Mercury* (18 March 1944), p. 13.

Other Items

Newspaper Reports:

"A Visiting Author," in an unsigned column "Between You and Me," Toronto, *Evening Telegram* (13 May 1942), p. 9.

"Notes on Books and Authors" in column "Between You and Me," Toronto, *Evening Telegram* (21 May 1942), p. 9.

"Toronto New Studio of Margaret Duley," *The Toronto Star* (16 May 1942), p. 10

"Newfoundland as a Country Very Little Known," St. John's, *Evening Telegram* (11 July 1942), p. 4. There appears to be a confused reference here. There is no mention of *Older than Eden* in the Macmillan file. The St. John's columnist may be referring to *Octaves of Dawn* submitted 7 January 1944.

Obituaries:

T. J. Duley: *The Evening Herald* (14 January 1920), p. 4; *The Daily News* (14 January 1920), p. 4; *St. John's Daily Star* (14 January 1920, p. 10; *Evening Advocate* (14 January 1920), p. 8.

John Clift: "Capt. John Clift, M. C.," *St. John's Daily Star* (12 February 1920), p. 1; "Death of Captain John Clift, M. C.," *Evening Advocate* (12 February 1920), p. 4; "Passing of John Clift, M. C.," *Evening Herald* (12 February 1920), p. 5.

Margaret Duley: "Newfoundland Novelist Margaret Duley Dies," *Daily News* (23 March 1968), p. 3

SKELETON GENEOLOGY

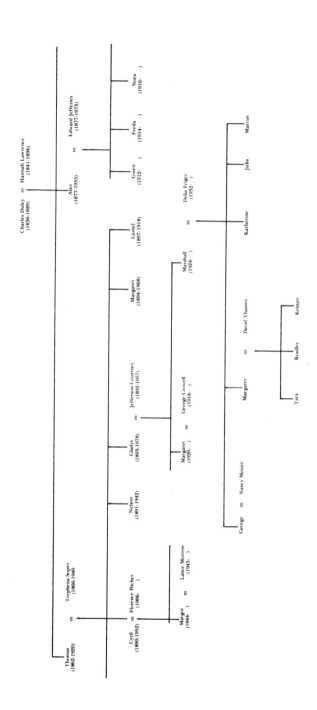

Margaret Duley

Books by Newfoundland Writers, from
HARRY CUFF PUBLICATIONS LIMITED

Georgiana Cooper, *The Deserted Island*
R. Augustus Parsons, *Curtain Call*
Percy Janes, *Light and Dark*
Albert Holmes, *A Boat of My Own*
Alastair Macdonald, *A Different Lens*
Harold Paddock, *Tung Tyde*
Allen Evans, *The Splendour of St. Jacques*
Tom Dawe, *Island Spell*
Edmund Hunt, *Aspects of the History of Trinity*
Percy Janes, *Newfoundlanders*
Tom Dawe, *The Loon in the Dark Tide*
Harold Horwood, *Tales of the Labrador Indians*
Irving Fogwill, *A Short Distance Only*
Tom Moore, *The Black Heart*
Jessie Mifflen, *"Be You A Library Missionary, Miss?"*
E.H. King (Ed.), *Choice Poems from the Newfoundland Quarterly*
Tom Dawe & Sylvia Ficken, *A Gommil from Bumble Bee Bight*
Elizabeth Miller (Editor), *The Best of Ted Russell, Number 1*
Cyril F. Poole, *In Search of the Newfoundland Soul*
Percy Janes & Harry Cuff (Editors), *Newfoundland Short Stories*
Kelly Russell, *Rufus Guinchard: The Man and His Music*
S. Robert Cooper, *Random Thoughts*
W. Kirwin (Ed.), *John White's Collection of Johnny Burke Songs*
Aubrey Tizzard, *Down on the French Shore*
Tom Dawe, *The Yarns of Ishmael Drake*
Stella & Linda Russell, *The Discontented Hippopotamus*
Wallace Bursey, *No Right of Spring*
Melvin Baker, *Aspects of 19th Century St. John's Municipal History*
Malcolm MacLeod, *Nearer Than Neighbours*
M. Baker, R. Cuff, & B. Gillespie, *Workingmen's St. John's*
Michael J. McCarthy, *The Irish in Newfoundland, 1623-1800*
Walter Peddle, *Traditional Furniture of Outport Newfoundland*
Ray Guy, *An Heroine for our Time*
Paul O'Neill, *The Seat Imperial: Bay Bulls Past and Present*
Cyril Poole, *The Time of My Life*
Alison Feder, *Mary Duley: Newfoundland Novelist*
A. Brian Peckford, *The Past in the Present*